THE

# ENNEAGRAM
# SPECTRUM
# OF PERSONALITY
# STYLES

25TH ANNIVERSARY EDITION

# THE
# ENNEAGRAM
# SPECTRUM
# OF PERSONALITY
# STYLES

## AN INTRODUCTORY GUIDE

### JEROME P. WAGNER, PH.D.

WITH A NEW INTRODUCTION BY THE AUTHOR

MEDIA

Published 2021 by Gildan Media LLC
aka G&D Media
www.GandDmedia.com

First edition published 1996, second edition published 2021.

Cover design by Tom McKeveny

Design by Meghan Day Healey of Story Horse, LLC

Library of Congress Cataloging-in-Publication Data is available upon request

ISBN: 978-1-7225-0522-6

10   9   8   7   6   5   4   3   2   1

# Contents

# Foreword

*by Helen Palmer*

I first met Dr. Wagner through a microfilm of his dissertation over twenty years ago—an academic treatment of the Enneagram material that has recently attracted a wide international audience. Since then, we've conferred, argued, agreed, and challenged each other's thinking, all of which has been immensely satisfying. Even when you don't see eye to eye with Jerry, his clarity always adds an interesting angle to the debate.

This workbook is his piece of the Enneagram magic that draws those who seek something more than Freud's agenda of good love and work as the apex of well-being. It's a really good guide and I'm delighted to recommend it to both new and longterm students who will benefit from his way of bringing the types to life.

—Helen Palmer
Teacher and author of *The Enneagram,*
*The Enneagram In Love And Work,*
*The Pocket Enneagram*

# Foreword

*by Thomas Condon*

Most introductions to the Enneagram reduce it to a collection of types, but this book takes just the right tone. It offers a dynamic version of the system that is rooted in common sense and personal experience.

The writing is distilled and precise, and Wagner's descriptions of personality styles reflect his own vocabulary and vision. Deep mastery of the Enneagram is hard-won and evident in the quality of insight presented here; the author has decades of experience and it shows.

I especially like the book's exercises. Simple yet profound, they point directly to the Enneagram's best purpose—unveiling our inner map of reality. Readers will find surprising new ways to apply the Enneagram both personally and professionally as well as a direct path to their personal depths. For these and many other reasons, this book is a pleasure to recommend.

—Thomas Condon
Author of *The Everyday Enneagram,*
*The Enneagram Movie & Video Guide*

# Introduction to the 25th Anniversary Edition

I t's hard to believe it's been twenty-five years since *The Enneagram Spectrum of Personality Styles* was first published. Much has changed since then, as looking at my old photo in the back of the original would attest. Just as the number of hairs on my head have diminished, so have the number of Enneagram books, articles, websites, inventories, and products increased.

The bibliography originally listed twenty-one books, seven articles, and eight dissertations. I will leave it to the reader to add up the number of entries in the new bibliography. And even this is incomplete.

I wrote my dissertation on the Enneagram in 1981. It was the first unpublished (as most dissertations are) description of the Enneagram system and styles. I was named an Honorary Founder of the International Enneagram Association in recognition of this contribution. As I said when I received the award, if you join something early enough and stay around long enough, you get a prize. I am honored in both meanings of the word.

When I researched my dissertation forty years ago, it was the third dissertation on the Enneagram and nothing was published outside of academia. The Enneagram was passed on through oral tradition and teaching. This led me to suggest to my dissertation committee that, instead of bibliographical citations, I put in phone numbers in the reference section so they could call up people and hear what they had to say about the Enneagram. Surprisingly they failed to see the humor in this but nonetheless let me proceed with my research. I am forever grateful to their farsightedness which allowed me to get out of graduate school.

When I first learned the Enneagram in 1971, we were cautioned to not speak about it until we were thoroughly familiar with the styles. That lasted about a week as it was very difficult to keep quiet about such a fascinating system. Since then much has been spoken and written about the Enneagram.

What is one to make of all this new material on the Enneagram? Was the Enneagram written in stone and so should be transmitted exactly as learned? This is the oral tradition approach where the student learned and memorized the material from the master and passed it on unaltered

Or is the Enneagram a living tradition that grows and diversifies and is open to ever new contributions and adumbrations? Is the Enneagram best optically viewed through a microscope or telescope where the vision is held steady? Or is it best optimally viewed like a kaleidoscope where new configurations appear with each turn?

And if there are new interpretations and refiguring being offered (which might be required to get your book published), how is one to evaluate the additions and accretions. If all theories are false or partial or not yet replaced, how does the listener/reader assess them?

Well, there are several validity sources.

One might appeal to **authority**. This is the dogmatic approach. Who said so?

One might appeal to **reason**. This is the rational approach. Does this make any sense? Is it logical?

One might appeal to **experience**. This is the romantic approach. Does this fit with my experience?

One might appeal to **science**. This is the empirical approach. Show me the data.

One might appeal to **usefulness**. This is the pragmatic approach. So what? Can I apply it?

One might appeal to **revelation**. This is the faith approach. What does God or some higher authority have to say about it?

One might appeal to **scripture**. This is the hermeneutic approach. Where is it written?

Depending on one's own philosophical or religious bent, one could use several or all of these validity sources. I come from a humanistic and scientific background so I tend to ask does this make any sense at all? Or is it so abstract and convoluted that I don't see how it applies to me? Which is a pragmatic question. Does it fit my experience? Or is it a completely made-up theory? (Well, actually, all theories are made up.) And where is the data? Did you sequester yourself in your room and just think great thoughts? Or did you interview people, ask them about their experience, and do some research to check out your hypotheses? While there has been much more research done on the Enneagram, more peer-reviewed empirical studies are needed to get the Enneagram into mainstream social sciences.

Many of the original Enneagram authorities have passed away since *The Enneagram Spectrum* was first published. Just this year Oscar Ichazo (who some call the father of the Enneagram) and Claudio Naranjo (sometimes called the mother of the Enneagram) died. My own teacher Robert Ochs, S.J. died a few years ago. Sadly we lost three of the Founders of the International Enneagram Association (IEA): Ted Donson, Don Riso and David Daniels. We also miss other wonderful contributors to the Enneagram: Suzanne Zuercher, Elizabeth Wagele, and others to whom I apologize for not remembering them as I write this. If you want to appeal to authorities, you can't do better than these.

When I first learned the Enneagram in the early 1970s, there was not much spoken and little written about the Enneagram style *subtypes*. In my original mimeographed notes (yes, I did say the early 1970s) there were about three sentences for each of the twenty-seven subtypes. And since the original *Enneagram Spectrum* book was an introduction to the Enneagram, I wanted to keep it simple and just present the nine basic styles. So, I left out the subtypes.

However, in the last few years there has been a growing interest in the subtypes as they do influence what the styles are preoccupied with and how they show up. Claudio Naranjo has recently written about the subtypes and offered workshops about them. Bea Chestnut and Ginger Lapid-Bogda have also written about the subtypes following Naranjo's new line of thinking. Mario Sikora reformulated the subtypes to make them more simpatico for a business community. Don Riso, Russ Hudson, Tom Condon, Peter O'Hanrahan, and David Daniels have also written and spoken about the subtypes.

So, to bring this *Enneagram Spectrum* edition into the twenty-first century, I will review some current thinking about the subtypes and provide brief descriptions of the twenty-seven subtypes in the Appendix (see page 167).

Since nothing in life, nor the Enneagram, is simple, we need to make some distinctions.

There are three centers; three instincts; and twenty-seven subtypes (which are a combination of one of the instincts and one of the nine passions/vices for each type.) If you haven't put this book down yet, let's continue.

## Three Centers

If I were to ask you "Where is your center?" What would you say? Some say my center is in my head, right behind my eyes; others say my center is in my heart or chest region; still others say my center is in my gut or my whole body. All are correct. We are three-brained beings with three centers of intelligence: IQ, mental; EQ, emotional; SQ, bodily. We are endowed with all three intelligences but we tend to prefer one over the others. At the end of the day, or consideration, or decision, we trust one a little more. Gurdjieff spoke of Man Number One, Man Number Two, and Man Number Three (he was nineteenth and twentieth century), each of which preferred one of the three centers. Man/Woman Number 4 integrated all three centers.

When it comes to making a decision, you might ask yourself: What does my head say about this? What does my heart say about this? What does my body say about this? If they are all in agreement, you will probably make a good decision that you will stick with. If you get two out of three in agreement, you might make a good lasting decision. If none of the centers agree, you might want to put off your decision, as a house divided against itself cannot stand. Lincoln did not know about the Enneagram as far as I know.

## Three Instincts

As organisms that have evolved over millennia, Mother Nature has equipped us with instincts to help us survive. We don't have unvarying pre-wired instincts like our animal ancestors. We don't build nests the same way each time. Just walk down your block and look at all the different houses. Nor do we have sex the same way each time. Just read the *Kama Sutra*. We do have some pre-wiring inherited from our predecessors, though, that incline us to react in certain ways. We have also evolved a consciousness that allows us to override our natural proclivities—sometimes for better; sometimes for worse.

Evolutionary psychologists say we all have a *self-preservation instinct* that helps us to individually survive. As herd creatures or social beings, our ancestors discovered that they survived better together than isolated and so gifted us with a *social instinct*. We all also have a *sexual instinct* that enables the species to survive. Thank you, Mom and Dad.

Instincts are healthy. If we don't interfere with them, they will lead us to what we need to survive and thrive. That's the good news. The bad news is we can corrupt even very natural processes. This happens when our passion, or vice, or maladaptive emotional schema leaks into our instincts and distorts them. Which leads us to the twenty-seven subtypes.

## Twenty-seven Subtypes

If you rely on authority as your validity check, know that Enneagram authorities disagree about the subtypes. They even disagree on what to call the three instincts. While there is a higher and lower intellectual center and a higher and lower emotional center, there are three side-by-side expressions of the bodily center.

Gurdjieff divided this somatic center into the *moving, instinctive, and sexual* centers.

Ichazo refers to the *social, self-preservation, and sexual* instincts.

The Enneagram Institute of Riso and Hudson refers to the instinctual variants of *self-preservation, social, and sexual*.

The Enneagram in the Narrative Tradition of Palmer and Daniels labels the subtypes as *self-preservation, social,* and *intimate* or *one-on-one.*

The Awareness to Action approach of Sikora renames them *preserving, navigating,* and *transmitting.*

When I first learned the Enneagram from Bob Ochs, S.J. who had just attended the seminar of Claudio Naranjo who had just returned from Chile having studied with Oscar Ichazo, I had the impression that the three subtypes had something in common no matter which style they accompanied.

I used the example of going to a conference. The *self-preservation subtypes* are concerned about surviving the conference. They check the weather in the area, the accommodations, the food, the safety of the surroundings, their travel arrangements, etc. The *social subtypes* are more concerned about who will be attending the conference, who they will be with. Will we be like-minded, have similar values and interests, have the same philosophy? Will I fit in and belong? The *sexual/intimate/one-on-one* subtypes will be able to relax when they connect with one other person at the conference. Or they may travel with a companion or visit a relative in the area.

I also described the energy of the subtypes as tentative, anxious, more introverted (*self-preservation*) or moderate, easy-going, relatable, ambiverted or more extraverted (*social*), or intense, forceful, strong, extraverted (*sexual*). Or, and it's a stretch, the subtypes are like the expressions of water: mist, hard to get hold of (*self-preservation*); water, adaptable to its surroundings and container (*social*); and ice, firm and tangible (*sexual*). I'm happy to let all that go.

We tend to live within one of the subtypes all of our life. This may be due to the interaction of temperament and environment, just like the types themselves. Or one theory postulates we are pre-occupied with certain issues because those needs weren't met when we were growing up.

It's also possible that, given your current circumstances, one of the instincts might become more salient. For example, if you lost your job, your self-preservation instinct might become figural. If you have just fallen in love, your sexual instinct might be more pronounced. If you have joined a new neighborhood, company, or protest movement, your social instinct would come to the fore.

Some speak of the stacking or prioritizing of the instincts—which is first, second, and third? or primary, auxiliary, or over-looked?

Ichazo said that when the vice of each style leaks into the three instincts of that style, a word arises to describe that state. So, he has twenty-seven words to describe that combination. But then he and others changed some of the words. So apparently the Enneagram subtypes are not set in linguistic stone.

Naranjo has also revised his understanding of the twenty-seven subtypes. They do not necessarily have the same dynamics for each of the nine styles. In the original thinking, if you were to put all the self-preservation, social, and intimate subtypes in their respective groups, each would have something in common even though they were different enneatypes.

The new thinking is that within the subtypes of each type, there is a *counter-type* whose expression seems out-of-sync with the flow of the major style. The energy is different and this subtype might actually appear like some other type entirely. Now we're back to our validity sources: what makes sense to you? what fits your experience (personal validation)? what do others say about their experience (consensual validation)? is there any data to support this position? et.al.

In the Appendix is my description of the subtypes that attempts to honor the most recent thinking. Recall that a subtype results from a mixture of the vice or passion (anger, pride, deceit, envy, avarice, fear, gluttony, lust, indolence) and the instinct (self-preservation, social, sexual) of the type.

Other authors have written and presented about the subtypes: Riso-Hudson 1999; Naranjo YouTube; Chestnut 2013; Lapid-Bogda 2018; Daniels 2019; Sikora mariosikora.com; Condon thechangeworks.com; Huertz 2020.

After all these years, I still find the Enneagram a comprehensive and useful psychospiritual system. I am heartened that a younger generation has taken it up and I look forward to reading and hearing their contributions.

# Introduction

I t is always fascinating and mutually confirming when theories and descriptions of personality from various sources of perennial wisdom resonate with contemporary psychological systems of personality. Such is the case with the Enneagram theory of the human person with its manifestations in nine personality styles.

The Enneagram is a nine-pointed figure in a circular setting that is used to display nine personality styles. (In Greek, *Ennea* means nine and *gramma* means point.)

This array has been compared to a wheel of colors. As you shine white light into a prism, it fans out into a spectrum of the basic colors. According to this metaphor, every person contains all the hues of the spectrum although one color particularly stands out or characterizes each individual. From a spiritual point of view, this metaphor says that Divinity descends and shows itself through nine earthly manifestations; from a philosophical point of view, it says that Being is disclosed through nine essential characteristics; from a psychological viewpoint, it states that human nature is expressed in nine natural fundamental ways.

The personality paradigms or patterns that are arranged in this circumplex model represent, depending on which metaphor you select, either nine manifestations of the Divine, or nine qualities of Being, or nine phenomenological world views and perspectives. From this latter point of view, these underlying fundamental schemas or maps are root organizing assumptions or core beliefs which influence and even determine our perceptions, thoughts, values, feelings, and behaviors. These paradigms are at the heart of how we think and feel about ourselves and other people and they govern the kinds of interactions with others we allow ourselves to think about and to have. These styles, then, are different ways of being in the world; different ways of experiencing, perceiving, understanding, evaluating, and responding to ourselves, others, and reality.

Traditional schools of wisdom often use a circle as a symbol of unity, completeness and fullness. So it is not surprising that a circular figure is used to describe the full range of human expression. Interestingly, modern psychology through complex statistical factor analysis has found that circumplex models are the most apt means for graphically plotting personality characteristics.

Although the origins of the Enneagram are disputed (some speculate its roots lie in antiquity; some trace its lineage to the middle ages; still others allege it is a modern discovery) and the exact transmission of the Enneagram symbol remains murky, what is clear is that the laws and descriptions of the human essence and personality as seen through the lens of the Enneagram have been recognized in some fashion across centuries as well as across races, cultures, age spans, and genders. There does appear to be something universal in the nature and functioning of the human person that is being expressed through this system.

Since it has become better known in the last twenty years, the Enneagram has become popular and is being validated in such varying cultures as Japan, India, Africa, Europe, North and South America. Today it is being used in a variety of settings from growth centers and therapy rooms to classrooms and business boardrooms with a variety of purposes from personal, psychological, and spiritual growth to couple interactions, team-building, and management effectiveness.

The Enneagram was originally transmitted through oral tradition and is probably best learned through hearing about it and interacting with others. Only in the last few years has the Enneagram been transcribed into written form for wider publication. This Introduction with its workbook and exercises is intended to be a bridge between the oral and written traditions. It can be used by workshop presenters, therapists, and consultants as a teaching aid for introducing the Enneagram to their clients. It can also stand on its own as a brief written primer for the Enneagram.

The exercises and descriptions that follow are designed to introduce you to the general personality theory that grounds the Enneagram and to familiarize you with the nine hues that make up its spectrum of personality styles. Hopefully this combination of experiential reflection and presentation of theory will help you locate, understand, and appreciate your own particular style.

This primer presumes no prior knowledge of the Enneagram. Complete the exercises in the Introduction, compare with your own style the word and phrase descriptors before each chapter, then consider the descriptions of the nine Enneagram styles.

The word/phrase descriptors are meant to be a *precis* or partial cataloging of the positive and negative features of the nine styles. For a formally researched, statistically reliable and validated inventory, with a standardized sample and normative scores, you can take the *Wagner Enneagram Personality Style Scales (WEPSS)* at www.wepss.com.

Like the *WEPSS*, the exercises have been developed over many years, through many workshops and courses. They are designed to help you reflect on your own experience. As you till the data of your experience, the Enneagram descriptions may expose a pattern that has been present in your life without your recognizing it.

The exercises begin with very general reflection questions and then become more specific, something like a funnel which is wide at the top and narrow at the bottom. There are exercises for each dimension of the Enneagram personality mosaic. So this manual follows the process of knowing. Begin with your *experience* to provide the data; then let *understanding* arise from your experience to produce a template for organizing the data;

then come to some *judgment* about your experience and understanding.

## Core Self or Essence or Objective Paradigm

Some schools of perennial wisdom (including the Enneagram) and some contemporary psychological theories of development and personality make a basic distinction between our *essence* or real self and our *personality* or public or false self. First we'll consider our natural, genuine core self—the self we were born with. Then we'll look at our public self—the protective covering around our true self that we donned and/or were conditioned into whose function is to protect our vulnerable self, keep it secure, and facilitate our commerce with our environment.

In our essence, at the heart of each style, lie certain strengths and capabilities that enable us to survive and thrive. We experience these abilities and qualities as values or ideals that we prize and are spontaneously drawn to. All of these values are virtually or potentially present in our core self, and we are capable of appreciating and actualizing all of them. Temperamentally, though, we tend to favor and are motivated by a hierarchy of these values, with one or a few being more potent and central than others. These values are the motivating and organizing tendencies that become central for each personality style. These *core value tendencies* organize and guide our energies, perceptions, emotional reactions, and behaviors. They are at the root of who we are and who we want to become.

The following exercises are designed to help you get in touch with your own core values. They are general inquiries into your fundamental attractions, orientations, meanings, and motivations. They are meant to reveal what is important to you, what really matters. Record your answers on a separate piece of paper or in a journal.

## Exercise 1:
### What is the purpose of life?

If a young child asked you what the purpose of life is—what are we here for—how would you respond to him or her? Remember, this is a young child (let's say around age six), so your response has to be simple and brief.

A variation of this theme would be to substitute a Martian for a child. The Martian asks you, as an Earthling, why you are on this planet. What is the purpose of Earthlings? What would you say to the Martian?

Take some time to reflect on this and record your answer.

## Exercise 2:
### If you only had one year to live, what would you do?

If you were told you only had one year to live, what would you do in that year? Your health will be fine all the way up to the end. Then in the last few weeks you will deteriorate rapidly and die. How would you spend the year?

An additional consideration you might ask yourself is why aren't you doing this now? Why not now?

**Exercise 3:**

**Write your own personal mission statement.**

What would you like or what do you understand your mission in life to be? This statement is meant to be the embodiment of your vision and values. This declaration will express what you believe the meaning of your life is all about.

Put another way: what is your vocation? What do you feel called *to be* and *to do*? What do you believe is the purpose of your life?

Write down your personal mission statement. Within it you will find expressed your innermost values and ideals (i.e., The kind of person I would like to be is_____; The kinds of activities I would like to engage in are _____; My personal mission is to_____).

**Exercise 4:**

**What do you really want?**

What do you *really* want in your truest self? Write down what comes to you.

With this material from your own experience and understanding, look now at Figure 1 (page 29).

Figure 1 summarizes much of the material that will be treated in discussing the nine Enneagram styles. Nine positive core characteristics or values are represented by the *innermost circle* (I) of Figure 1. These values are part of our essence. The healthy self has the potential for valuing, developing, and utilizing each of these characteristics. When one of these qualities is present, all are virtually present, for each contains the others. For example, if you cultivate the valued characteristic of goodness, you will also be loving, wise, loyal, and the rest. Pictorially, this is indicated by the dotted lines showing these core values as permeable and intermingling.

You will find these values described in more detail under the heading *Positive Core Value Tendencies* the left hand column of each of the nine styles. If you compare your responses to Exercises 1, 2, 3, and 4 to the descriptions in this column, you may find some resonances to your own value preferences. The adjectives and phrases in the top section of each checklist titled *Positive Descriptions of Your Style* also point to the healthy characteristics found in the authentic self.

To operate effectively in the world, we need, and have available to us, all of these qualities. So in a situation when we need to be assertive, we can call on our power; when we need to be nurturing, we can call on our love; when we need to have fun, we can call on our joy, etc. The flexible person has this whole spectrum of adaptive attitudes and behaviors available. Even so, we naturally tend to rely on and use one or a few favorite ways of operating. By temperament or destiny we are particularly attracted to, are guided by, and cultivate one of these value vectors which becomes an organizer and expresser of the self. The other vectors are used as auxiliaries to complement our central preference.

We need all nine paradigm perspectives to see reality objectively. The healthy person has access to these reality based and reality informed paradigms which provide pliancy and flexibility to our style. To be effective, we

# Enneagram Personality Style Profile

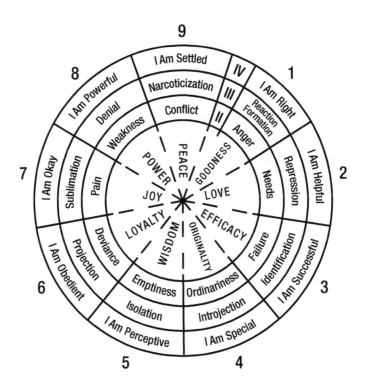

I   Genuine Ideal or Authentic Values
II  Area of Avoidance
III Defense Mechanism
IV  Idealized Self-Image or Compensating Values

figure 1

need to take multiple perspectives on a problem or situation. Even so, we tend to see the world from one favored and developed perspective or another. This is the particular viewpoint, acumen and problem-solving approach we have to offer any group. Due to our expertise in our paradigm, we can often perceive and understand some things more clearly than others; we are more competent in some areas than others; and we can resolve certain issues more easily than others. When we are acting from our healthy self, we contribute our strengths, gifts, and points of view to society.

## Personality or Public Self or Subjective Paradigm

Under favorable inner and outer conditions and with good enough parenting, our core real self emerges and flourishes. When our spontaneous urges, sensations, feelings, images, and ideas are met with empathic interest, acceptance, and encouragement, we then develop according to the enfolding of our essential nature. We become who we really are.

However if the appearance of our core self is met with indifference, criticism, or misinterpretation, then we develop a personality or public self to cover our real self and protect it. This peripheral self is an attempt to defend and maintain our inner self in the face of our critics, to appease them, to gain their attention and approval, to win them over to our side, or to defeat them. These strategies are attempts to make ourselves attractive, good, acceptable, safe, and secure. Instead of *express*ing our real values, preferences, feelings, and thoughts, we try to *impress* others. We begin to manipulate both ourselves and others. We become what we believe we *have* to be.

Our core gifts get distorted and caricatured into ways we think we *should* be. To be acceptable or somebody, we *have* to be good, giving, efficient, special, etc. Our core ideals or values become crystallized into *idealized self-images,* partial expressions of our full self that we over-identify with and believe represent our whole self. We mistakenly believe that if we attain and manifest these idealizations, they will gain for us positive reinforcement or at least help us avoid negative reinforcement. Now we use our gifts and strengths to protect ourselves from others rather than to build up our community.

Our paradigms or perspectives on the world tend to become static, rigid, and inflexible. Our perspective becomes more limited and narrow and we develop tunnel vision. Our paradigms become distorted and subjective instead of reality-determined. We try to solve problems in the same stereotyped manner with the same automatic interpretations and reactions.

In sum, when we lose touch with our core self, we need to substitute something in its place. So we assume a personality and pursue substitute or compensating values in an attempt to fill in what feels missing.

Exercises 5 through 15 may help you discover your personality or subjective paradigm. These exercises explore the remaining three rings in Figure 1: your idealized self-image, an area you tend to avoid, and the defensive techniques you employ to help you avoid whatever doesn't fit your image of yourself.

## Exercise 5:
### How have you survived?

In this "dog-eat-dog world," what advice would you give to a young child about how to survive? How do you make it in this cruel world? What kind of survival tactics and strategies have you discovered and devised that have kept you safe. For example, some people might suggest: "Get them before they get you." Others might say: "Be nice to people." While others might advise: "Get out of town or hide out."

Again, you may substitute a Venusian for a young child. Here the Venusian is asking how do Earthlings survive on this inhospitable planet? How have you managed to live this long?

Make a list of your techniques.

## Exercise 6:
### Where have you been looking for what you want in the wrong places?

What have you substituted for what you really want that you wrote down in Exercise 4? As the song says, are you looking for love in all the wrong places (like in food, drink, or sex)? Or are you looking for truth through status? Etc.

Write down what you have settled for or have mistakenly been seeking.

Our idealized self-image or compensating values are represented by the *outermost* circle (IV) in Figure 1. These idealizations tend to be caricatures or exaggerations of the essential values and characteristics found in our real self. These personality styles lie around the periphery of our self where they act as a covering to protect the self and act as mediators or translators between the self and the world. These styles can vary in how flexible or stifling they are—and they vary in how well they translate or convey to the world who we really are and in how distorted or undistorted they bring in to us what is in the world. These strategies are demarcated by solid lines, indicating the rigidity and impermeability of the characteristics of our personality. The farther removed we get from our core self, the more stereotyped and automatic our thoughts, feelings, and behaviors become. The more set we are in our ways, the less the perspectives, approaches, and strengths of the other styles are available to us.

You will find these defensive or survival strategies for each of the nine styles spelled out more fully in the column entitled *Distorted Core Characteristics*. There you will see how our healthy strivings can become distorted when we over-identify with and overuse our basic gifts. Compare the survival techniques you cataloged in Exercises 5 and 6 with the ones listed here and see where you might recognize yourself.

# Area of Avoidance

Parts of ourselves we consider unacceptable, embarrassing, or intolerable because they don't fit our idealized self-image are disowned and relegated to our unconscious or are projected onto others. The result is that we lose touch with even more aspects of ourselves. Our response repertoire becomes more limited and, ultimately, we are less effective. The opposing attributes, polarities, or antitheses of our self-image, then, are found in our area of avoidance.

Each personality paradigm is like a lens or a searchlight with a particular focus and clarity. Those aspects of reality that lie outside the territory scanned by our paradigm are often vague, obscurely recognized, or not seen at all. Just as our paradigm enables us to see some things more clearly than others might, so we can miss or pass over realities and possibilities because we're not looking for them, are looking the other way, or don't want to see them.

Exercise 7:

### Me and Not-Me

Make two columnar lists. In the first column, write down all the characteristics you associate with yourself. These are qualities that you identify with, find acceptable, and place inside your self boundary.

In the next column, write down the opposite characteristics of the qualities you listed in the first column. These are the polarities you find unacceptable and don't want to identify with and so place outside your self boundary. You may repress these characteristics so they appear in your dreams as shadow figures. Or you may project them onto other people so they appear as traits you don't like in others or as traits you admire in others. You can project out or throw away your strengths as well as your weaknesses.

For example, in Column 1 (Me) you may have written: "I am nice." In Column 2 (Not-Me) you might write: "I am cruel," or whatever the opposite of nice might be for you.

In the first column (Me) you may have said: "I am fearful," or "I seek security." While in the second column (Not-Me) you may have said: "I am brave," or "I am adventuresome," or whatever the polarity of fearful and security-seeking is for you.

## Exercise 8:
### Re-owning the Not-Me
Go back to your list of characteristics in Column 2 and identify with them or re-own them. For example, how are you cruel? Or brave? Resist your initial reaction of saying "I'm not," and search out areas of your life where you have or do now manifest these qualities. They represent untapped energy and strength. If you can access them, they will broaden your paradigm considerably and give you more resources for handling situations that arise.

## Exercise 9:
### Re-framing the Not-Me
If you're still having trouble identifying with some characteristics in your Not-Me column, take each quality

and think about what good is in that characteristic. For example, what's good about being cruel? Or what good qualities are contained in being cruel? Perhaps these good qualities are being distorted. For example, there might be considerable strength contained in the anger and aggression found in being cruel. If this strength and energy can be tapped cleanly, you can use it productively.

## Exercise 10:
## What are you afraid of?

What fears stand between you and your real self? What are your fears that are keeping you from doing what you really want to do?

What is the demon or dragon that guards the path to your inner self? When you quiet yourself and attempt to get in touch with yourself, what arises to distract you or block your view?

Make a list of all the things you are afraid of.

## Exercise 11:
## How do your fears keep you trapped in your false personality or ego?

Often we become stuck in our habitual patterns of thinking, feeling, and behaving because our irrational and no longer helpful fears get in the way of trying something new and different.

For example, do you always have to be nice and accommodating because you are afraid of expressing your anger or your opinion for fear that people will not like you?

Or do you always have to be working on some project for fear that if you slow down or have nothing to do, some uncomfortable feelings or wishes may arise in you? Or are you afraid there will be no one there when you finally come home to yourself?

Consider the fears you cataloged in Exercise 10. Notice how they keep you imprisoned in your recurring reaction loops, and determine whether these fears are still realistic or mostly mythical by now.

## Exercise 12:
### Where are the edges of your paradigm?

Does your own paradigm create certain perceptions, interpretations, rules, limits, boundaries, or taboos that keep you fearful?

For example, if your paradigm involves perfectionism, then your rules say you have to be right all the time and you fear being wrong or not doing something perfect enough. Someone with a different paradigm won't be bothered nearly as much about being right or exact. Or if your paradigm says you have to look calm, cool, and collected in order to survive, then you "can't" express your feelings and you are afraid of them and stay away from them. On the other hand, someone else can express their feelings freely, but they're not allowed to think straight.

Paradigms involve strong beliefs, and when you come up to the edge of your belief, it can be very frightening to go any farther. For example, if you believe the world is flat, when you come up to your horizon you won't want to go any further.

So, if you believe you have to be strong, then you might be afraid of and avoid being weak.

Write out how your paradigm creates your fears and avoidances and how the rules of your paradigm prohibit you from doing what you legitimately might want to do.

### Exercise 13:

**If you break this rule or taboo or cross this boundary, what are you afraid will happen?**

Taboos or idols have power because you make yourself afraid of them.

What are you telling yourself or what have you been told happens to people who possess this dreaded quality or who manifest these terrible characteristics? What will happen to you if you go too far?

What happens to people who get angry? Are they shunned, abandoned, locked up?

What happens to people who are lazy? Do they turn out to be bums? Or do they end up like your Uncle Harry or your older sister?

Are the consequences specific ("You'll be sent to the insane asylum") or vague? ("You'd better not do that, or else!")

Write down what you are afraid will happen if you enter your area of avoidance.

### Exercise 14:

**What do you need to do to stop worshiping this idol? What do you need to cast out this fear? What**

**resources do you need to marshal to confront your fears?**

Perhaps you need to turn around and confront your fear. Maybe all dogs (or men or women) don't bite. Expose yourself to the very thing you are afraid of. You may be surprised to discover that you survive.

Perhaps you need to upgrade your information or get information you lack. Sex may not make your hair fall out or permanently stain your soul. The information you initially received which made you fearful may have been faulty.

Perhaps before you say goodbye, you may first need to reassure yourself that you will have connections in the future. Or before you make contact, you may need to feel the inner strength to be able to break that contact and withdraw when you need to.

You may need to rally some inner allies before you face your fears and/or you might want some outer friends and guides around when you push through your fear barrier. You don't necessarily have to do all it by yourself.

Write down the strategies and resources you already have and those you may need to acquire.

This land of shadows or area of avoidance is represented by circle II of Figure 1. Notice that it lies between the core self and the personality. The most direct route to the self is through this avoided territory. To find ourselves we need to look at, identify with, reclaim, and repatriate these banished features of our self. The way to wholeness is through honoring and integrating all of our polarities, not through cutting off half of them. Holding onto both ends of our polarities creates energy; letting go of one end depletes energy.

You will also find a section describing the *Area of Avoidance* under each of the nine Enneagram styles. Compare these with your own avoidances you discovered in Exercises 7–14 and *see* where you recognize yourself.

## Defense Mechanisms

As we approach our area of avoidance, we become anxious. So we devise ways to keep these unacceptable aspects of ourselves out of our awareness. The defense mechanisms act as buffers between our *persona* or idealized self and our shadow characteristics or avoided self. Whatever we consider to be *I* is allowed inside our paradigm or personality boundary and is granted access to our awareness. What we think of as *Not-I* is placed outside our paradigm boundary and is banished from consciousness. Our defenses prevent these rejected aspects of ourselves from entering the province of the personality. Unfortunately, they also keep us from contacting and re-owning these parts of our core self.

Exercise 15:

What are your defense mechanisms?

This is a difficult question, because if your defense mechanisms are working properly, you won't be aware of them—so you need to be patient and observe yourself carefully.

When you start to feel anxious, what happens next? What do you do?

When you vaguely become aware of something in yourself you are uncomfortable with (like feeling angry, afraid, sexy, etc.) or if someone else brings up something you are uncomfortable with, what do you do to avoid it? For example, do you distract yourself or change the subject? Do you go blank and lose your train of thought, stop feeling, numb out, tighten your muscles, or hold your breath?

Do you go into your head and get too heady? Or do you lose your mind and get too feeling? Or do you just act impulsively without much thought or feeling?

Do you blame others and start finding fault with them?

Do you do the opposite of what you really want to do? If you want to do something for yourself, do you do what you *should do* instead? Or if you want to slug someone, are you nice to them instead?

Do you repress or deny what seems to be quite obvious to others?

You probably have many defense mechanisms at your disposal. We need them to survive psychologically. Write down the ones you rely on the most.

The defense mechanisms are found in circle III of Figure 1, between the idealized self-image (circle IV) and the area of avoidance (circle II). Graphically, the defense mechanisms separate what we identify with as ourself from what we avoid as antithetical to our self. Psychically, they serve the same buffering function.

You will also find a characteristic *Defense Mechanism* described under each of the nine Enneagram styles. Notice whether any of the defenses you discovered in Exercise 15 match any of these.

## Objective Principles and Paradigms/ Adaptive Cognitive Schemas

Just as our physical body has certain laws and principles by which it operates, so does the psyche have certain laws within which it functions optimally. As the body has certain tolerances or limits within which we must stay or we damage the body (i.e., our body temperature can only go so high or so low or we might die), so does the psyche have certain boundaries that need to be respected or we injure the psyche (i.e., we can only tolerate so much injustice, unloving, ugliness, etc., before we become sick in our spirit or demoralized.)

When we are living in accordance with our core authentic self, we have an intuitive, though perhaps unconscious, understanding of these objective principles or natural laws. Our paradigms or inner maps are accurate reflections of reality and are reliable guides for our choices and behaviors because they are aligned with the laws of the universe and with the laws of our own human nature. We function most effectively when we live in harmony with these universal principles. They are built-in to lead us to self-realization, to self-transcendence, and to communion with others and the world.

These objective principles and paradigms are found in the *inner* circle of Figure 2 (see page 46) where they reside in our essence or real self. These attitudes are delineated by dotted lines, indicating their mutual co-presence and influence. That is, each of these principles implies and virtually contains all the others. For example, when freedom is present, there is also hope, justice, love, etc.

Schemas represent patterned ways of thinking, feeling, and behaving. Adaptive cognitive schemas faithfully record, code, and organize external and internal data, so our cognitive maps are accurate reflections of the territory. They are formulated on repetitions occurring in the real world. They are adaptive because they enable us to realistically negotiate our way around in the world.

You will find these objective paradigms or adaptive schemas described under the heading *Adaptive Cognitive Schemas* for each of the nine Enneagram styles. Each style has a particular principle that is especially useful to remember and operate out of so the person remains aligned with reality and her or his own true nature.

### Exercise 16:
### When you are in a resourceful state, what beliefs are in place that align you with reality?

When you hold and express certain beliefs, attitudes, and assumptions, you will find your body feeling physically relaxed, supple, strong, and energetic. You will experience genuine emotions such as joy, sadness, anger, fear, etc. Your mind will be dear, open, and expansive.

Since it might be difficult to uncover these underlying objective paradigms or principles, work backwards. Recall a moment when you felt at home and at ease in your body, when you spontaneously felt and expressed some feeling, when you were attentive, alert, clearheaded and single-minded, when you genuinely felt connected to yourself and others; in short, when you were fully present in the here and now.

In this resourceful state, what adaptive beliefs did you have about yourself, about others, about the world and your place in it?

Record your underlying perceptions, beliefs, and principles.

## Subjective or Distorting Paradigms/ Maladaptive Cognitive Schemas

When we lose touch with our core self and lose faith in our inner and outer reality, we fashion our own vision and version of reality. Our narrowed and inflexible paradigms or faulty assumptions and belief systems are inaccurate maps which limit and distort our perception of reality. They are not trustworthy guides since they lead to the self-defeating strategies of the personality (though they were originally hoped to be self-protecting and enhancing). When we follow these disordered perceptions, feelings, and behaviors, we are on the path away from our core self and away from genuine contact with others.

Maladaptive schemas impose archaic patterns on reality. They recreate and then perceive old repetitions and recurrences where there may not be any. They are maladaptive because these maps don't fit the contemporary territory but rather distort incoming information to fit old patterns.

These illusory paradigms or perceptions and their ensuing limited strategies are found in the outer circle of Figure 2, next page, where they reside in the periphery or *personality*. These stances are separated by solid lines, indicating their narrow focus and tunnel vision. These positions often exclude other points of view.

You will find these distorting paradigms spelled out under the heading *Maladaptive Cognitive Schemas* for each of the nine styles. Each style has a particular trap or maladaptive schema that keeps the individual stuck in a recurring reaction loop.

**Exercise 17:**

**When you are in a non-resourceful state, what are the distorted perceptions and inaccurate interpretations that are in place then?**

When you hold beliefs and assumptions that are not aligned with your own true nature or with reality, you will experience your body being tense, rigid, enervated or hyperactive; you will experience contaminated feelings such as guilt, depression, hostility, envy, greed; your mind will be distracted, closed, cluttered, confused.

Remember a time when you felt disconnected from yourself and from others, when your body felt anxious and tense, when your emotions felt crabbed or numbed or out of control, when your mind couldn't focus or when

# Adaptive and Maladaptive Cognitive Schema of Each Personality Style

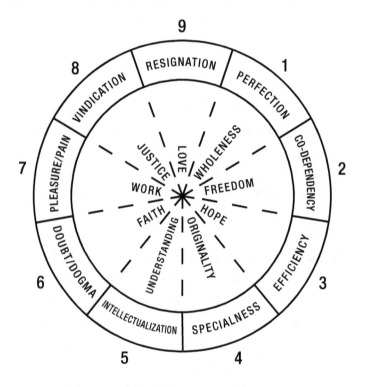

CORE (inner circle) =
Adaptive Schema/Objective Paradigm

PERIPHERY (outer circle) =
Maladaptive Schema/Distorting Paradigm

figure 2

you couldn't get it off something; in short, when you were in the "there and then" instead of in the present.

When you were in that non-resourceful state, what were your maladaptive beliefs about yourself, about others, about the world and your place in it?

Write down the perceptions, assumptions and convictions you were holding then.

## Virtues/Adaptive Emotional Schemas

Virtues are good habits (*virtus* means strength in Latin). They are the strengths that accompany a fully functioning and developing human being. They are clear, undistorted, objective expressions of spiritual energy. When we are living in accordance with our real nature or essential self and our paradigms, assumptions and perceptions are accurate and objective, then a corresponding virtue flows naturally from this position. For example, the virtue of courage flows naturally from a sense of faith and trust in our own and others' inner nature.

Virtues are adaptive emotional schemas that emanate from our essential nature and represent dispositions that manifest our best self. They are attitudes best suited to help us connect and harmonize with reality and to energize, fulfill, and transcend our real self.

The *inner* circle of Figure 3, next page, displays the virtues of each type. They are the endowments of our essence. They are separated by a dotted line, indicating that when one of the virtues is present, all the others are in effect contained within it.

# Adaptive and Maladaptive Emotional Schema of Each Personality Style

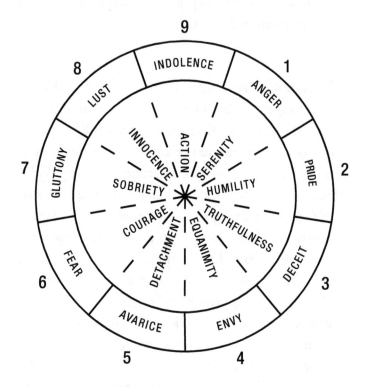

CORE (inner circle) =
Adaptive Schema/Virtue

PERIPHERY (outer circle) =
Maladaptive Schema/Passion

figure 3

You will also find a characteristic *Virtue or Adaptive Emotional Schema* detailed in the left hand column for each of the nine Enneagram styles. Just as each style has a particular objective principle or adaptive cognitive schema to align you with and remind you of your true nature, each style also has a distinctive virtue or guiding force and attitude to keep you on your true path.

## Exercise 18:
## What are the virtues or strengths or good habits needed for living a balanced adult life?

In your opinion, what skills and dispositions does a person need to live in an adult manner?

For example, what interpersonal or social skills should a person cultivate and possess? What intellectual, emotional, physical, moral, spiritual competencies does a person need for a sense of adult efficacy and mastery? Write out your list.

Look at the nine virtues presented for the Enneagram styles. Did any of them surprise you? Did you leave any of them out of your list? You might want to add them.

Considering all the virtues and skills mentioned, which ones do you already possess and are adept at?

Which habits and skills are you missing or deficient in?

What is interfering with your possessing and developing these virtues? For example, do you have some prohibition or inhibition about being strong? or loving? or feeling? or humorous? or intelligent?

You might also want to look ahead to the next section. Perhaps there is some bad habit or passion in place and operating that prevents the virtue from appearing and functioning.

## Passions/Maladaptive Emotional Schemas

Passions are bad habits. They are distorted expressions of spiritual energy which try to substitute for the virtues. Passions fuel and inflate the personality but do not nourish our core self, so we never feel really satisfied after exercising or giving into them. A self-defeating cycle gets established between our distorting paradigm and idealized self-image and the ruling passion. The idealized self-image inevitably gives rise to the passion which in turn urges us to pursue the automatic thoughts and behaviors of the personality. So each of the nine subjective paradigms produces its characteristic passion. For example, the pursuit of perfection, wherein we compare everything to unattainable ideals and then attempt to reach those ideals, leads to resentment because nothing appears as right or as fair as it should be. This anger and resentment then drive us to try harder to be perfect. Just as we tend to have only one idealized self-image, so each of us tends to have a basic ruling passion or vice.

Passions are maladaptive emotional schemas since they arise from the false self or personality, represent our non-resourceful self, and don't lead to satisfying contact between our real self and the world.

The passions and virtues are mutually opposing. If, in the presence of your passion, you simply observe it and don't act on it, then you experience your virtue. For example, if you feel greedy, but don't grab, then you are practicing the virtue of detachment.

Because the passions are associated with the peripheral self or personality, they are found in the *outer* circle of Figure 3. They are represented by solid lines since the passions tend to operate in a blind and inflexible manner with a tunnel-vision urgency.

The *Passions or Maladaptive Emotional Schemas* are also delineated in the right hand column (across from and opposed to the Virtues) for each of the nine Enneagram styles.

Exercise 19:

### What passions are in possession of you?

The passions are experienced as an addictive energy. They feel like alien forces that drive you and that seem out of your control.

What are the addictions and urges of your personality? What are you driven to thinking and feeling and doing that you know really isn't good for you? For example, do you compulsively compare yourself to others? Do you feel possessed by resentment or vengeance that you can't (or won't) let go of? Do you *have* to have something and feel desperately bad if you missed it?

Write down your addictions, compulsions, obsessions, blind urges, desires, thoughts, judgments, etc. Then compare these with the passions described for the Enneagram styles and note any similarities.

**Exercise 20:**
## What is your predominant fault?

According to perennial wisdom and many religious traditions, the passion was referred to as your predominant fault or cardinal sin since it was from this source or "hinge" that all your other misdirected attitudes and behavior flowed or were connected.

Do any of the passions or addictions you noted seem central to your personality style? Do any of these mal-energized attitudes seem to cause most of your problems? Do you recognize any of the passions as being pervasive throughout your personality or paradigm distortions?

Consider how this passion influences your perceptions, choices, and behaviors. Trace the tendrils of this passion throughout the fabric of your personality. Like the roots of a weed, you need to see how it stretches out and touches much of what you do.

For example, if your predominant passion is gluttony, you might note how your desire for new and varied experiences to spice up your life, your need to have your options open and commitments contained, your fear and avoidance of pain, etc., are all manifestations of your basic predominant fault or passion.

Write down your reflections and observations about your predominant fault.

# Paradigm Shifts

The following exercises are designed to help you reflect on changes in your perceptions, feelings, and behaviors. You may experience these shifts either as voluntary choices or involuntary movements. Hopefully you will gain some insights into how to vary your customary manner of interacting. The next exercise proposes the fundamental paradigm shift query.


**Exercise 21:**

**What is impossible for you to do within your own style? What can't you imagine yourself doing (i.e., if you could or would do it, it would fundamentally change your style)?**

A paradigm shift takes you outside of your own boundaries and into another paradigm or worldview with a new set of rules and boundaries.

What you find difficult to do might be relatively easy inside another paradigm. If your paradigm makes it difficult for you to express your feelings, another paradigm might make it natural and expected. If your paradigm makes expressing anger difficult for you, another's paradigm might make it facile. Or if your paradigm makes clear thinking difficult, another paradigm will find it the logical thing to do.

Some problems can't be easily solved by your paradigm but can be solved by someone else's paradigm. You can find the answers to some of your "unsolvable problems" by applying someone else's paradigm.

For example, do you find it hard to imagine yourself doing first what you want to do and then second what you *should* do? Or vice versa?

Do you find it almost inconceivable that you would express your feelings openly as you are feeling them?

Does it seem unimaginable to you to live without doubts?

Write down what you can't do (or, really, won't allow yourself to do)—something which, if you were doing it, would be a radical change in your style of living and interacting.

## Exercise 22:

### What happens to you under stressful conditions?

Do you find yourself regressing to earlier patterns of behavior? Do you find yourself thinking, feeling, behaving the way you did when you were little?

Do you try other desperate measures to avoid dealing with your issues?

Or under stress do you sometimes rise to the occasion and surprise yourself by how well you cope under pressure or in an emergency? Do you rally resources in yourself you usually don't call up?

Write down what you're like when you fall apart under stress. What are you thinking, feeling, and doing when you start to disintegrate? When stress brings out the worst in you, just what is that worst?

Write down what you're like when you pull yourself together under stress. How do you respond gracefully under fire? What are your effective coping strategies when you're under pressure? What are you thinking, feeling, and doing when you rise to the occasion?

## Stressful Conditions

Under stress, each style tends towards certain backup strategies of defense and coping. When our customary automatic paradigms and emotional and behavioral patterns fail to remedy the situation, we often compulsively use them more rather than try something different. When we finally give up on these patterns, or when they break down, we find ourselves by default using the compulsive maneuvers of another style.

### Shifting to the Low Side of the Proceeding Style

This regressive backup strategy can be identified by following the direction of the arrow *forward* from our customary style to the *proceeding* style. We begin to take on and resemble the negative features or the *low side* of this type. Besides assuming the compulsive strategies of this style, we also start to shim the same aspects of reality this type avoids. Thus even more parts of ourselves become unavailable and our reactions become more narrow and rigid. For example, the sensitive person despairs of trying to be special, begins to avoid his or her own needs, and instead attempts to help others as a way to gain love and attention. S/he becomes a "suffering servant." This would be how Style 4 might move toward the low or compulsive side of Style 2 when experiencing inner and outer stress.

**Shifting to the High Side of the Proceeding Style**

Stress often brings out the worst in us. However, sometimes it brings out the best. Under these circumstances, we find ourselves deliberately choosing the alternate paradigm and effective methods of another style. We can shift to the *high side* of the proceeding style. For example, the sensitive person, realizing s/he is becoming overly self-absorbed or involved in her own process, elects to go out of herself and genuinely empathize and serve others. This would be how Style 4 under stress might move toward the high or healthy side of Style 2.

These paradigm shifts toward regression, fragmentation, and compulsion or toward growth, integration, and wholeness are diagrammed in Figure 4, opposite.

Look at the section *Paradigm Shifts You May Experience Under Stressful Conditions* for each of the nine Enneagram styles and see where you recognize some of your own pattern shifts under stress.

### Exercise 23—What are you like in relaxed, nonthreatening situations?

When you are at your best, how do you *think* and *feel* about yourself, about other people, and about the way you can interact with others? How are you different here from when you feel anxious, threatened, or bad about yourself? What do you *do* when you are at your best that you can't or won't do at your worst?

When you feel safe (for example in your home environment or with your family) what do you allow yourself to think, feel, and do that you don't allow yourself to do in

# Paradigm Shifts

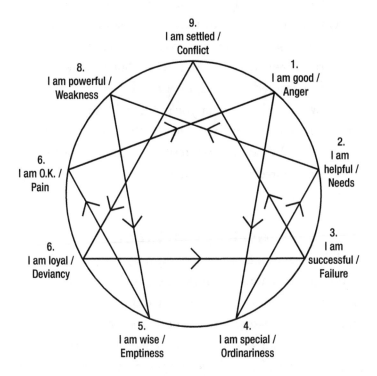

## Movements Toward Resourceful
## and Non-Resourceful States

figure 4

public? For example, are you more demanding or whining at home? Sometimes in familiar, comfortable settings, we allow our less sociably acceptable parts to come out.

Under relaxed conditions either some suppressed strengths or some covered up weaknesses may emerge.

Write down what you're like at your best when you feel safe, accepted, relaxed, integrated, free, and alive.

Now write down what you're like when you feel safe and unthreatened and you let out the little gremlin or devil in you. What uncharacteristic or unsocial behaviors do you let yourself get away with?

## Healthy Conditions

Under relaxed, affirming conditions, each style tends toward more balanced, integrated, objective, proactive (vs. reactive) modes of perception and behavior. To remedy a situation, we *give in* to another approach instead of *giving up* on our customary approach. This represents a paradigm shift. We enlarge our perspective with another frame of reference and increase our behavioral repertoire with another set of skills.

### Shifting to the High Side of the Preceding Style

This alternate paradigm and strategy is found in the healthy coping patterns of the style *preceding* our own, going *backward* against the direction of the arrow. We begin to assume and activate the positive features or *high side* of this type. To discover the underutilized resources in ourselves, we can look to the perspective, strengths, effective coping strategies, and attitudes of the preceding style to know what to draw upon in ourselves to get balanced or unstuck. It is generally healthy and motivating to be able to acknowledge and activate the idealized self statement of the preceding type. For example, it is beneficial for the perfectionist style to be able to say, "I'm okay even though I'm not perfect."

### Shifting to the Down Side of the Preceding Style
Sometimes when we are in relaxed comfortable surroundings we can slip into the *down side* of the preceding style. We miss the mark and take on the compulsive features of the other paradigm. We do things in our family that we wouldn't dare do in public. For example, when feeling safe, the wise person might become bossy or cruel (the low side of Style 8) instead of acting out of their instincts and being assertive (the high side of Style 8).

These *paradigm* shifts toward growth, integration, and wholeness or towards stagnation, fragmentation, and compulsion are diagrammed in Figure 4.

Look at the descriptions of the *Paradigm Shifts You May Experience Under Relaxed Conditions* for each of the nine Enneagram styles and see where you recognize your perceptual, emotional, and behavioral shifts when you feel accepted and safe.

## Three Centers or Instincts
According to some schools of perennial wisdom, each person has three centers of intelligence or three loci of

decision making or three instincts that help us survive and thrive in the physical, interpersonal, and spiritual realms in which we live. Modem neuroanatomy has uncovered three layers in the evolution of the brain. There is the reptilian brain located atop the brain stem. Next developed the old mammalian brain consisting of the limbic system which encircles the reptilian brain. Finally there evolved the neocortex which surrounds the mammalian brain.

The ***instinct for self-preservation*** is located in our gut center in the pelvic basin and provides us with a *physical sense* of how we are doing in relation to ourselves. It naturally informs us about what we need. When this instinct is ill-functioning or damaged, we experience a deep insecurity about ourselves. This is called the *Kath* center. In traditional wisdom, it is the place we go to get centered and still. It is also the center of movement as in Tai Chi and the martial arts. Various breathing, movement, and postural exercises are used to activate this center. In the reptilian brain are found those brain functions responsible for breathing, coordinating and smoothing movements, along with other autonomic nervous system activities. This section of the brain is said to contain the ancestral lore of the species.

The ***instinct for interpersonal relations*** is located in our heart center and provides us with an *emotional sense* of whom we are with and how we are doing in relationship to others. It tells us what the other person needs. When this instinct is not functioning, we experience a sense of loneliness. This is called the *Oth* center. In-traditional wisdom, this is the center of devotion and love. The heart center is often activated by chanting or other auditory practices such as vocal prayer. The old mammalian brain contains those parts of the brain that regulate the emotions along with the pleasure/pain center.

The ***instinct for connection and orientation*** (syntony) is located in our head center and provides us with an *intellectual sense of* where we are, where we have come from, and where we are going. This instinct helps us find a sense of direction, purpose, and meaning. When it is damaged, we feel unconnected, useless, and inadequate. This is called the *Path* center. In perennial wisdom, the head center is activated through visualization techniques. This is the seat of enlightenment. The neocortex or gray matter is also called the associative cortex because it is able to make associations, plan ahead and consider consequences, delay and inhibit, make voluntary movements and carry on discourse with the external environment.

While each of us has and needs all three centers, we typically rely on and prefer one center over the others. Enneagram Types 8-9-1 prefer the *gut* center; Types 2-3-4 prefer the *heart* center; Types 5-6-7 prefer the *head* center. When one center tries to do the work of the other centers, we often become imbalanced and become too heady or too feeling dominated or too impulsive. When all three centers are allowed to function freely and work in harmony, we experience a sense of wholeness, integration, and balance.

Plato and later Gurdjieff spoke of three types of individuals in whom either the head, heart, or abdominal centers predominated. A fourth type of person was one who had integrated all three centers. Plato used the image of a winged chariot pulled by horses and driven by a charioteer to describe the interrelationships among the physical center (the chariot), the emotional center (the horses), and the intellectual center (the charioteer). Gurdjieff updated this image to his time and spoke of a carriage, horse, and driver to illustrate the three centers.

These three centers for gathering, evaluating, and acting on information are depicted in Figure 5.

The remaining exercises ask you to reflect on your experience of your three centers.

## Exercise 24:

### Which is your preferred center: head, heart, or gut (body)?

When you need to make an important decision, which center do you ultimately consult and trust?

Do you consult and trust logic and reason? Do you list the pros and cons of the various options available to you? Do you take a rational approach to decision-making? Do you use your head?

Do you consult and trust your emotions to discern how you feel about your various options? Do you imagine the possibilities available to you and let your feelings move you one way or the other? Do you use your heart?

Do you consult and trust your body to give you a felt sense for what you want? Do you make decisions rap-

# The Three Instincts

## Intellectual Center
Orienting instinct "Where am I?"
Purpose, direction
Dysfunction: Feels useless, inadequate

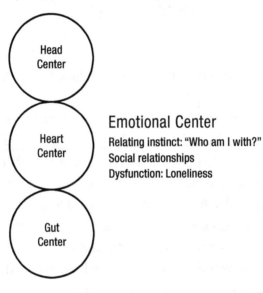

## Emotional Center
Relating instinct: "Who am I with?"
Social relationships
Dysfunction: Loneliness

## Instinctual Center
Conserving instinct "How am I?"
Self preservation
Dysfunction: Insecurity about self

figure 5

idly and instinctively, sometimes before you think or feel anything about your options? With this judgment there seems no room for doubt. Do you use your gut?

Write out how you characteristically make important decisions in your life. You may find you use all three approaches. The more the better. But which center is your final "go ahead with it" arbiter?

## Exercise 25:
## What is the condition of your carriage (physical center) at this time?

Have you taken care of your body or carriage? Is it polished and well-oiled and ready for the road of life? Or have you neglected it so it is rusty and can barely move?

Through exercise and movement, your muscles and joints naturally lubricate themselves. Do you regularly exercise to keep your body in tone?

Are you overweight so your horses can barely pull you? Or are you underweight to such an extent that you can't bear any burden placed on you?

Do you need to consider your diet? Are you providing your body the vitamins and minerals it needs? Or are you clogging up your arteries? If your body craves proteins, do you give it the nourishment it needs or do you feed it cotton candy?

Are addictions to food, drink, chemicals, smoking, etc., substituting for healthy bodily care?

Do you need to pursue any body therapies to get your carriage in shape (therapeutic massage, Rolfing, bioenergetics, Feldenkrais movement therapy, Reichian therapy, Reiki therapy, Tai Chi, Aikido or other martial arts, breathing therapies, Zen or other methods, to name just a few, for reaching your still point)?

Write down your reflections.

**Exercise 26:**

**What is the condition of your horses (emotional center) at this time?**

What is the status of your emotional life? Have you developed your emotions to the extent you have developed your mind and body? Are you in touch with and comfortable expressing the full range of your feelings?

How are you with your *hard feelings* such as anger? Are you able to move against others with assertive and confrontational behavior?

How are you with your *soft feelings* such as love, affection and joy? Can you move towards others with warmth?

How are you with your *fragile feelings* such as sadness, embarrassment, and fear? Can you move away from others when appropriate? Or express your vulnerability?

Are your horses underfed and underexercised? Do you provide them with energy and oxygen? Or do you cut them off by holding your breath and tightening your muscles? Are your feelings overcontrolled, restricted, repressed, compulsive?

Or are your horses wild and undisciplined? Do your feelings run wild so they are in control of you instead of you providing a gently guiding rein? Are your feelings hysterical, labile, overwhelming, impulsive?

Again, are any addictions (food, alcohol, nicotine, chemical substances, people, work, etc.) substituting for, covering over, or distracting you from genuine emotional contact and expression?

Do you need to consider any emotional cathartic therapies to free your emotions? Examples include Gestalt therapy group therapy Primal Scream or other regressive therapies.

Write down how you are with your feelings.

## Exercise 27:

## What is the condition of your driver (head center) at this time?

What is the status of your cognitive life? The fanciest carriage with the liveliest horses won't do you any good if your driver is drunk or doesn't know the way.

Are your cognitive maps, your belief systems, your assumptions, your ways of construing and interpreting reality accurate and up to date? Or are you still working with the beliefs, attitudes, and maps you developed when you were a child? Do you need to update your maps?

Have you checked your assumptions out with other people lately? And have you checked your hypotheses and schemas against both external data and the data of your own experience? You may be changing the data to fit your schema or denying your own experience to fit some "should" or prejudice passed on to you when you were young.

Is your thinking clear or muddled? Are you engaging in "Stinkin' Thinkin'" as the Twelve-Step program calls it? Do you overgeneralize, absolutize, think in all-or-nothing, either-or, black-or-white categories? Do you minimize or ignore the data in front of you? Do you confuse your projections with reality?

Does your attention habitually go in a certain direction? or in a self-defeating cycle? Do you need some form of cognitive therapy to get your thinking up-to-date, accurate, and realistic? Rational-Emotive therapy, cognitive-behavioral or cognitive dynamic therapy, aspects of Neurolinguistic Programming, and Multi-Modal therapy are a few examples.

Write down your assessment of how your head center is functioning.

An earlier exercise (3) asked what you really wanted in your truest self. The remaining exercises ask you to be more specific and reflect on what each center of your self desires.

**Exercise 28:**
**What does your head need and want?**

**Exercise 29:**
**What does your heart need and want?**

**Exercise 30:**
**What does your gut (body) need and want?**

# The Nine Styles

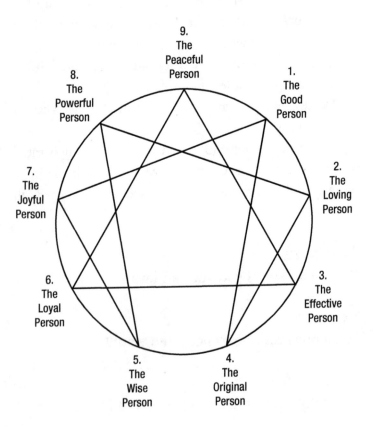

# Style 1
## The Good Person

### Positive Descriptors of Your Style

serious

responsible

dedicated

conscientious

high purpose

precise

punctual

honest

hardworking

moral

high standards

striving for excellence

idealistic

reliable

thorough

painstaking

fair

persevering

develop all potentials

ethical

clarity seeking

intense

### Negative Descriptors of Your Style

overly critical

demanding

angry

uptight

sharp

driven

impatient

slave-driver

moralistic

trying too hard

perfectionistic

high expectations

unrealistic

overly-persistent

strict

interfering

puritanical

preachy

many "shoulds"

overly serious

## Positive Core Value Tendencies

You value and are attracted to *goodness*. You want to make the world a better place to live in. You want to realize all of your potentials and help others actualize theirs.

You have an appreciation for and a dedication to excellence and doing things well.

You have an ability to see how people or situations could be and you are willing to work hard to bring about that reality.

You have a highly developed critical faculty and so are good at quality control.

You have the ability to be exact, to get the correct point. You have a clarity of focus and intention. You like to be precise.

## Distorted Core Characteristics

You can overidentify with the *idealized self-image* of being *good, right, or perfect*. These become more important than anything else. If you are a good girl or good boy, then you are acceptable.

You are afraid to do anything unless you can do it perfectly.

You have difficulty accepting yourself, other people, and reality as it is.

You can become preoccupied with what is wrong or missing and consequently may not appreciate what is actually there.

You can become pedantic about what is right. You can get overly preoccupied with details and with getting everything right. You can become obsessive or compulsive.

## Positive Core Value Tendencies

You are altruistic and have an idealistic concern for people and causes beyond yourself.

You desire, are committed to and take action to bring about a better world.

You have strong feelings about and become intensely involved in whatever you value.

You are conscientious, dedicated, persevering, reliable, hardworking, and industrious.

You are serious. You live your life with high intentions, ideals, and purpose.

You have an appreciation for fairness and justice.

## Distorted Core Characteristics

You may not consider your own needs, wants, and feelings as important as what you think you *should* do.

You have a tendency to interfere with or to intrude upon others' lives to make them better—for their own good.

You can be overzealous. You can be unwilling to see another point of view. You have difficulty stepping back and being dispassionate.

You can become over-responsible and a workaholic. You become tense and live your life under pressure with time running out to do all the good that must be done.

You can take yourself and situations too seriously. You develop an inability to play and have fun.

You are prone to resentment since you tend to readily judge that life isn't fair.

## Positive Core Value Tendencies

You have a strong moral character. You try to live your life true to a higher good and a higher vision. You want to live a life of moral purity.

## Distorted Core Characteristics

You can be moralistic and puritanical. You are tyrannized by your *shoulds*.

## Objective Paradigm
*Wholeness*

**Adaptive Cognitive Schema:**

You understand perfection to be a *process*, as something you will always be on your way towards.

You trust the growth process in yourself and others. The universe is unfolding as it should.

You can appreciate the moment as it is. You enjoy yourself and others as dappled. You are right now just where you ought to be.

## Distorting Paradigm
*Perfection*

**Maladaptive Cognitive Schema:**

You think of perfection in terms of a finished *product*, as something you should have achieved yesterday.

You set your own unreachable standards because you don't trust your natural unfolding and development.

You believe you need to improve upon the moment. The better is the enemy of the good. Instead of leaving yourself, or others, alone, you interrupt and interfere by trying to make it better.

## Virtue: *Serenity*

**Adaptive Emotional Schema:**

You are in touch with and are at ease with yourself. You are able to relax in the process of living. You experience the balance and harmony between opposites.

## Passion: *Anger*

**Maladaptive Emotional Schema:**

Anger can become an habitual emotional attitude for you. You are resentful because nothing meets your high standards and your expectations aren't fulfilled. You engage in all-or-nothing, black-and-white thinking. Either it's perfect or it's no good at all.

**Area of Avoidance:** *Anger*

You are uncomfortable being angry and find this feeling unacceptable even though it is a frequent reaction of yours. Good boys and girls should not be angry.

**Defense Mechanism:** *Reaction Formation*

To keep your angry impulses out of your awareness, you do the opposite of what you are inclined to do. For example, instead of confronting someone, you are nice to them; or instead of being sexual, you become puritanical.

### How the Distortion of This Style Developed

- You were rewarded for being good and doing the right thing; you were punished for being bad and doing bad things.
- You got approval by being a good boy or good girl.
- You developed the belief that you were "somebody" if your ideals were higher than everybody else's, and you were "nobody" if you weren't perfect.
- You believed that by seeking excellence and having high standards you would be better than others.
- Being an over-achiever brought you good feelings and social approval.
- You came to believe that others wouldn't like you unless you were perfect.
- You discovered you could do things better or do things right if you did them yourself.

- You learned to control yourself and others and the situation by following the rules and prescribed *shoulds*.
- You were given, or you assumed, responsibility at a young age. You were expected to grow up early and be a parent to your siblings and maybe even to your own parents.
- You may have been the eldest or an older child.
- You learned at home or at school that being angry was unacceptable.


**What You Miss as a Result of the Distortion of Your Style**

- Spontaneity; fun; lighthearted gaiety.
- More carefree interactions with people.
- Trust in yourself, others, reality.
- Going with the flow; enjoying the process instead of controlling and pushing the river.
- Feeling relaxed.
- Tolerance and acceptance instead of being under the gun, scrutinized, criticized, pressured.
- Being yourself instead of having to prove yourself.
- Living the unexamined life.
- Doing something half-well just because you like to do it or because it's worth doing even half-well.

## Paradigm Shifts You May Experience
## Under Stressful Conditions

### A Shift to the Low Side of Your Own Style

- You may try even harder to right the situation or make yourself better.
- You might strive more, push more, work more—to the point of exhaustion.
- You may become more rigid and strict with yourself and others.
- You may get more resentful because your goodness isn't fairly recompensed. You are good, you try hard, and you don't feel rewarded; and that isn't fair.
- You might become more serious, angry, frustrated, morose, and depressed.

### A Shift to the Low Side of Style 4

- You may feel misunderstood, victimized, taken advantage of. You may feel bad because the world doesn't appreciate your efforts to make it better.
- You might attempt to be *special* if you can't be right or perfect enough.
- You may become more critical of yourself sometimes to the point of saying: *"What's the use. I'm hopeless. I'll never be good enough."*
- You may turn your anger on yourself and become depressed instead of channeling your energy into productive problem solving.

- You may give up on your precision and exactness and begin to exaggerate the situation and become overwhelmed by your feelings. You avoid ordinary experience and become dramatic.
- You may engage in *stinkin' thinkin'* by absolutizing and catastrophizing and by getting stuck in the polarities of either/or; black/white.
- Instead of taking action and doing something about what's wrong, you may become demoralized and immobilized. You may find yourself mired in melancholy and self-pity.
- You may get discouraged and give up on your ideals and goals.
- You may avoid looking at and dealing with reality in a straightforward, no-nonsense manner and become manipulative.

### A Shift to the High Side of Style 4

- Here you get into your real feelings. You get in touch with your real preferences and identity and disidentify with your external and internal "shoulds" and expectations.
- You go in search of your real self instead of trying to realize your idealizations.

## Paradigm Shifts You May Experience
## Under Relaxed Conditions

### A *Shift to the High Side of Your Own Style*

- You become forgiving of yourself and others.
- You accept yourself and the situation as it is instead of being critical and immediately wanting to change something. You let the weeds grow with the wheat. You accept yourself as dappled.
- You practice the Serenity Prayer and are more tolerant and patient.
- You shift your categories from either/or and all-or-nothing to both/and, continuum, process.
- You can ask yourself what you're angry about and check whether your expectations for yourself and others are unrealistically high.
- You express your anger cleanly or let it go instead of holding onto it and remaining resentful.
- You are more accepting of all your feelings—especially your sexual and aggressive responses. What you think are demons are actually *daimons* (friendly helpers).

### A *Shift to the High Side of Style 7*

- You can say to yourself *"I'm okay even though I'm imperfect."*
- You take yourself and the situation less seriously. You get in touch with your playful side. You take a break before you break.

- You are more spontaneous. You let yourself go and let things happen instead of trying to get more control.
- You lighten up instead of getting more heavy and serious. You take your foot off the brake when you're skidding vs. pushing on the brake harder.
- You can go with the flow instead of against it. You don't push the river since it flows by itself. You trust the process. Everything, including you, is on the way.
- You can ask the child in you what she or he needs and wants.
- You can do what is desirable and pleasurable instead of what *should* be done.
- You use divergent vs. convergent thinking. There are many ways to solve a problem vs. only one right way. You are more creative and imaginative.
- You look at what's right in yourself and the situation instead of what's wrong. You can look at what's there vs. what isn't there. You can see the glass as half-full just as well as half-empty.

### A Shift to the Low Side of Style 7

- You may try to escape the present pain or situation through addictions or other pleasurable trapdoors (e.g., you may try to avoid your inner voices and "shoulds" through addictions to alcohol, drugs, sex, etc.).

# Style 2
## The Loving Person

## Positive Descriptors of Your Style

helping

unselfish

giving

sensitive

complimenting

caring

loving

nurturing

gentle

sympathetic

affirming

accepting

sacrificing

other-centered

compassionate

listening

praising

serving

relationship-oriented

supporting

## Negative Descriptors of Your Style

intrusive

interfering

possessive

manipulative

demanding

victim

rescuing

complaining

guilt-inducing

nonconfronting

unwilling to receive

overprotecting

martyr

other-directed

needy

smothering

infantilizing

undeserving of help

jealous

overly sweet

| Positive Core Value Tendencies | Distorted Core Characteristics |
|---|---|
| You value and are attracted to *love*. You want to make the world a more loving place to live in. | You can overidentify with the *idealized self-image* of being *loving* and *helpful*. You are acceptable only if you are loving and nice. |
| You are naturally a giving, generous, helpful person. You enjoy giving to others. You are generous with yourself, time, energy, and possessions. | You can become a compulsive helper. You give love to gain attention and approval. You expect appreciation in return for your care. |
| You are supportive, nurturing, and considerate. | You can be overprotective and infantilize others to like you by giving strokes to get strokes. |
| You spontaneously appreciate, approve, applaud, and praise others' gifts. | You can manipulate others to like you by giving strokes to get strokes. |
| You have the ability to build people up and make them feel good about themselves. | You have difficulty expressing your negative feelings such as anger and disappointment and confronting things you don't like in others. |
| You are gentle and kindhearted and work toward establishing harmony and reconciliation. | It's hard for you to be assertive and/or angry. You can overdo trying to please others. |

| Positive Core Value Tendencies | Distorted Core Characteristics |
|---|---|
| You have an intuitive sense for what others need, want, and are feeling. | You can be out of touch with your own needs, wants, and feelings. |
| You are sociable, friendly, and approachable. Relationships are what life is all about for you. | You get anxious when you are alone. You may not know how to relate except through helping. Curiously enough, you may fear intimacy. |
| You enjoy helping others grow and supporting them. | It is difficult to leave others on their own, to let them grow up—or to let them fall down. |
| You are a good listener. You listen with your heart and are nonjudgmental. | You are prone to giving advice. You desire to control others by being helpful. You want to be important in someone's life because of all you've done for them. |
| Your sense of worth comes from yourself. You are filled with love from the inside out, like a wellspring. | Your worth comes from being needed and from others' approval. *I am somebody if I'm needed.* Love comes from outside in to fill you. |
| If someone is hungry, you teach them how to fish so they can feed themselves. | If someone is hungry, you give them a fish so they will need to return to you to be fed. |

## Objective Paradigm
*Freedom*

**Adaptive Cognitive Schema:**

You understand freedom to mean living within the natural laws and limits of giving and receiving.

You are interdependent; it is more blessed to give *and* to receive.

You are responsive to the unfreedom in others. You are able to set others free.

## Distorting Paradigm
*Codependence*

**Maladaptive Cognitive Schema:**

You believe freedom means being free from needs and being free from needing others' help.

You are codependent; it is more blessed to give *than* to receive.

You yourself are enslaved by caring for others to gain self-worth, and you bind others to you because they need you.

## Virtue: *Humility*

**Adaptive Emotional Schema:**

When you experience humility, you accept your own limits and boundaries. You are able to say *no* as well as *yes*. You are able to take time out for yourself.

## Passion: *Pride*

**Maladaptive Emotional Schema:**

You are proud when you believe you have unlimited resources to give. You believe you don't need or don't deserve help. You are liable to burn out.

**Area of Avoidance:** *Personal Needs*

You have difficulty getting in touch with and accepting your own needs. You are either not aware of them at all or else you don't want to burden others with your needs. You are afraid you can't be a helper and be needy at the same time.

**Defense Mechanism:** *Repression*

Because your own needs make you anxious, you keep them out of your awareness by repressing them. You project your needs onto others (so other people are needy, but you aren't).

## How the Distortion of This Style Developed

- You got approval for helping and giving and not asking for much for yourself.
- You learned how to be sweet, funny, cute, and charming to get attention and to win affection.
- You received appreciation for your kindnesses.
- You became needed and important to people by helping them.
- You were made to feel guilty and to believe you were selfish if you expressed your own needs or cared for yourself.
- You discovered that to survive you needed to figure out what the other person wanted and then provide for their wants.

- You found that changing yourself to meet others' needs was preferable to remaining true to yourself and to your own needs.
- You had to provide emotional support for your parents—sometimes to the point of becoming the parent in your family.
- What *you* wanted or really needed wasn't empathized with or inquired about.
- You got rewarded for empathizing with others and making them feel better.
- You found that *moving toward* others in affection worked better for you than *moving against* others with anger or assertion or *moving away from* others by detaching yourself.
- You survived by being dependent on others' approval and by making yourself needed by them through your service.
- You experienced that pleasing others worked better than pleasing yourself.

## What You Miss as a Result of the Distortion of Your Style

- The joy of receiving without having to earn what you have been given; the experience of grace.
- Letting others feel good by giving to you.
- A sense of worth based on who you are vs. what you can give.
- The inner freedom that comes from an inner sense of approval and security vs. seeking approval from the outside.

- The experience of intimacy in a reciprocal relationship.
- Being really known by someone else, including your needs and vulnerabilities.
- The experience of self-expression vs. self-renunciation or effacement.
- Freedom in relationships where you don't have to be in control through helping.

## Paradigm Shifts You May Experience Under Stressful Conditions

### A *Shift to the Low Side of Your Own Style*
- You may increase your helping activity, still not get the appreciation you think you deserve, feel victimized and a martyr, and then reproach others for not caring for you more.
- You might try to get people to feel guilty to manipulate them to approve of you and appreciate you.
- As you approach burnout and exhaustion, you may become irritable, depressed, resent others' expectations, and wonder what it's all about.

### A *Shift to the Low Side of Style 8*
- You may become vengeful and vindictive (at least in your fantasies) toward those who don't appreciate you enough.
- You may become a persecutor instead of a rescuer.

- You may lose touch with your natural gentleness, become tough and develop a hard shell to protect your vulnerable self esteem.
- You may become bitter, jaded, and distrustful of others.
- You may cease helping others (for the time being) and tell them they're on their own.
- You may try to get others to be dependent on you so you can have power and control over them.
- Instead of asking for help, you may attempt to be more independent and refuse to need others. You may avoid not only your own needs, but any form of weakness.
- You may become less open to others and to yourself.

### A Shift to the High Side of Style 8

- You may get in touch with your real inner power and be genuinely free of your need for others' approval and appreciation.
- You may establish stronger self boundaries, claim your own autonomy stand on your own two feet, and not alter yourself to gain others' affirmation.
- You may take responsibility for your own needs and leave others responsible for their needs.
- You may express yourself honestly and forthrightly instead of trying to please others and say what you think they want to hear.

## Paradigm Shifts You May Experience
## Under Relaxed Conditions

### *A Shift to the High Side of Your Own Style*

- You find sources for your self-worth in other places besides helping.
- You get in touch with your *own* needs, wants, and feelings.
- You give yourself permission to take time for yourself and take time alone for yourself.
- You develop a consistent self that doesn't alter to meet others' wishes and needs.
- You can negotiate with others as an equal. You are not only good at helping others express their needs but you can also make sure your own needs are represented and heard.
- You can ask others for help directly vs. indirectly through helping them. You can make straightforward demands on others for what is rightly due you.
- You exercise self-care. You do what you need to do for yourself. You deserve to care for yourself, and you deserve to be cared for.
- You take a realistic accounting of your assets and limitations and own both of them. This is what humility means for you.
- You say "no" when you mean "no" and "yes" when you mean "yes."

- You let others take care of themselves. You take responsibility for your needs and let others take responsibility for their needs.
- You give because you want to rather than because you need appreciation and approval in return.
- You let yourself receive from others. You can let others gift you.

### A Shift to the High Side of Style 4

- You can say to yourself, *"I am special and so my needs are as important as anyone else's."*
- You get in touch with culture and beauty.
- You develop your creative, self-expressive side (vs. being self-effacing). You can egress your needs through creativity.
- You get in touch with your own unique identity and feelings and inner space. You get in touch with your sadness and regret over abandoning yourself in the service of others.

### A Shift to the Low Side of Style 4

- You may take on a pretentious, artistic image instead of a genuine expressive spirit.
- You may become petulant and demand that others appreciate you and recognize your specialness.

# Style 3
## The Effective Person

### Positive Descriptors of Your Style

efficient

successful

get things done

motivator

enthusiastic

pragmatic

practical

goal-oriented

energetic

manager

popular

active

dynamic

multi-faceted

organized

self-assured

marketer

industrious

team-builder

competent

### Negative Descriptors of Your Style

mechanical

get ahead

calculating

impatient

expedient

workaholic

chameleon-like

scheming

popularizer

image-conscious

self-promoting

appearances

jet set

success-driven

slick

political

misrepresenting

overachiever

role-playing

ignore feelings

## Positive Core Value Tendencies

## Distorted Core Characteristics

You are attracted to and value efficiency, productivity, industriousness, and competence.

You can overidentify with the *idealized self image* of being *successful* and *productive* such that your worth depends on what you do instead of who you are.

You possess a natural organizational ability.

You can become overly efficient, machine-like, and ultra-programmed.

You have the ability to get things done.

You may substitute projects for persons.

You make a good salesperson. You exude confidence and competence and so people are willing to buy you and your product.

You can become a *marketing personality*. Your worth depends upon how well you can sell yourself or how marketable you are.

You make a good team person. As a team leader, you are able to organize, run, and motivate a team. As a team member, you can carry out your own responsibilities.

You can lose your personal identity by conforming to the group image or to the image of what the group wants you to be.

You are a good energizer. You have the energy to accomplish things and you are able to motivate others.

You always have to be on the go. You are unable to slow down or you're afraid to relax. You believe that *progress is our most important product.*

## Positive Core Value Tendencies

## Distorted Core Characteristics

You are friendly, gregarious, and sociable.

Your relationships can be utilitarian and superficial.

You have an intuitive sense for what people expect. You instinctively know what image to present to be successful.

You may sell out and lose your personal self for the sake of a public mask.

You are adaptable. You can negotiate and compromise to get things accomplished.

You can be chameleon-like. You may betray your inner self for the sake of a role and compromise.

You are optimistic, enthusiastic, and self-confident.

You may deceive yourself and others by only portraying a successful image.

You have the capacity for hard work. You have tremendous enthusiasm for projects and goals.

You can become a workaholic. You exhibit Type A behavior. You perform and achieve in order to get approval.

## Objective Paradigm
*Hope*

**Adaptive Cognitive Schema:**

You can trust that all will run smoothly even when you're not working. You trust and have hope the world won't stop when you do.

You operate in harmony with natural life processes and within the social and natural laws.

## Distorting Paradigm
*Efficiency*

**Maladaptive Cognitive Schema:**

You believe that the smooth running of the organization or operation or cosmos depends mainly on your interventions.

You believe you are above the law. Your own operating rules are more efficient than universal principles. You may come to believe that the end justifies the means.

## Virtue: *Truthfulness*

**Adaptive Emotional Schema:**

You are truthful to your own inner self, feelings, and desires.

Your outer image matches your inner reality.

You are honest and loyal to others.

## Passion: *Deceit*

**Maladaptive Emotional Schema:**

You lose touch with your real feelings and wants and present programmed, planned feelings instead.

You can deceive yourself and others into believing that the image presented is your real self. You live out of an image vs. out of real emotional preferences.

You show others what you think they want to see or what looks successful.

**Area of Avoidance:** *Failure*

The area you are out of touch with and avoid is failure. You want to present an image of success so you hide anything that may appear less than successful or you reframe happenings in your life (i.e., you say, "There are no failures in life; there are only learning experiences").

**Defense Mechanism:** *Identification*

To keep failure out of your awareness, you identify with whatever successful mask or role you are playing at the time. You identify with your role instead of with yourself.

### How the Distortion of This Style Developed

- You were rewarded for your achievements rather than for yourself.
- Your worth depended on what you did instead of who you were.
- You were loved for what you produced or for the status you achieved.
- Playing a role was safer and got you further than being yourself.
- Performance and image were rewarded in place of emotional connections and deep involvements with others.
- You may have been a precocious child who got approval and attention by being successful at what you did, but you lost touch with your own feelings and preferences.

- Success, winning, getting ahead, and looking good were all emphasized in your family.
- Being the way other people wanted you to be got you what you wanted. You learned how to perform instead of how to be.
- Being efficient, organized, goal-oriented, and hard-working got you ahead of others.
- Programming yourself and being adaptable helped you to survive.

## What You Miss as a Result of the Distortion of Your Style

- The security that comes from knowing your worth is based on your self instead of your productions.
- Knowing your value doesn't depend on market conditions, i.e., what others expect of you now.
- The experience of being appreciated for yourself and not for your achievements.
- Being yourself, expressing yourself, letting others know you without having to filter yourself through a role or mask.
- Not being afraid of failing; detachment from success; doing something because it's worth doing whether it's successful or not.
- Feeling your own feelings vs. replacing them with performance.
- Being the master of your work instead of being mastered by your work.
- The ability to relax and let others run things or let the universe run itself.

- Emotional involvement with others resulting from the meeting of two real selves; genuine intimate relationships.

## Paradigm Shifts You May Experience
## Under Stressful Conditions

### A *Shift to the Low Side of Your Own Style*

- You may work harder, be even more on the go, take on more projects, shake more hands, put out even more press releases on yourself and your projects.
- You may become more concerned about your image and may imitate other roles or models instead of expressing yourself.
- You may doubt your self-worth and whether you really do have anything to contribute.

### A *Shift to the Low Side of Style 9*

- Besides wanting to avoid failure, you may also try to avoid conflict, both inner conflict and conflict with others.
- Instead of dealing with the pain or the problem, you may avoid it, procrastinate, distract yourself, or numb yourself.
- You may replace or numb your real feelings with more work.
- You may give up on your natural efficiency and problem-solving abilities and say, *"What's the difference"* or *"What's the use, it doesn't matter."*

- You may doubt yourself instead of trusting your genuine inner responses and desires.
- You may seek solutions from outside yourself vs. from within your own self and potentials.
- You may turn off your smooth running machine and go to bed. You go from on to off, from exertion to exhaustion.
- You may become resigned to how things are rather than trying to change them.
- You may turn to alcohol, drugs, eating, etc., if success and work don't seem fulfilling.
- You may become even more neglectful of your real self.

### A Shift to the High Side of Style 9

- You slow down to allow your real feelings and preferences to arise.
- You become more introverted and reflective and let your inner self develop.
- You become more contemplative and receptive to balance your activity.
- You can be at one with another in a self-forgetting manner.
- You are more at peace with yourself and less driven.

# Paradigm Shifts You May Experience
# Under Relaxed Conditions

## A *Shift to the High Side of Your Own Style*

- You save some energy for the development of your self instead of putting it all into your image or projects.
- You resist changing how you present yourself just to manipulate others.
- You are more honest. You discover your real feelings and tell the truth about them instead of exhibiting what you think you should feel in your role. You consider any lying to be a form of addiction.
- You accept failure as part of your life vs. blaming it on someone else or calling it something different (a learning experience, a partial success, etc.).
- You no longer act so mechanically and efficiently. You can drop out of the rat race.
- You can trust that the universe is running smoothly and on schedule and it can get along without you from time to time.
- You want to manifest and actualize what is real and worthwhile vs. the image that society rewards.
- You discover your lost child and develop the real you. You can separate yourself from your image.
- You want to work for society and the common good. You work for the benefit of others and not just to be successful.
- You allow yourself to get in touch with your physical sensations (i.e., fatigue).

*A Shift to the High Side of Style 6*

- You are loyal to yourself and others instead of to your products. *"To thine own self be true."*
- You are trustworthy as well as competent. This combination makes a good leader.
- If you believe in something, you stay with it even though it may not be socially applauded and popular. If it's worth doing, you do it even though you may fail.
- You can egress doubts. You no longer have to be competent about everything.
- You cooperate with others vs. compete with them. You trust that others can get things done.

*A Shift to the Low Side of Style 6*

- You might become even more obedient and conforming to external expectations.
- You could become even more of a company man or woman.
- You might lose yourself in some authority figure or guru.
- You might experience fear and panic as you relax and come back to yourself.

# Style 4
## The Original Person

## Positive Descriptors of Your Style

sensitive

classy

original

creative

intense

refined

making beautiful

intuitive

involved

nostalgic

caring

aesthetic

good taste

cultured

distinctive

expressive

feeling

questing

quality

## Negative Descriptors of Your Style

special

snobbish

up and down

eccentric

aloof

mourning

dramatic

controlling

exaggerating

attention-demanding

possessive

shifting emotions

complaining

standoffish

precious

elite

high-strung

overly-sensitive

clinging

misunderstood

## Positive Core Value Tendencies

## Distorted Core Characteristics

You are highly individual and value *originality*. You put your personal touch on everything you are involved in.

You can overidentify with the *idealized self-image* of being *special* and *unique*. You may become an eccentric caricature of originality.

Like a poet, you have an ability to make the ordinary extraordinary. You can take what is plain and make it special, like an oyster changes a grain of sand into a pearl.

You believe you must be unique, original, different; otherwise you are nobody. Your identity and worth depend on your being *special*.

You value and appreciate *beauty*. You want to make the world a more beautiful place. You have a highly developed aesthetic sense.

You can become an aesthete and artificially cultivate an artistic sensitivity. You can make a cult of art and beauty as an escape from mundane life.

You have an innate sense for quality. You have good taste and class.

You can look down on others for their philistine tastes. You may consider others to be tacky.

You are creative and imaginative. You favor creative channels of expression.

You believe you are so sensitive and your experience is so deep that mere words can't express it.

| Positive Core Value Tendencies | Distorted Core Characteristics |
|---|---|
| You are highly intuitive. You are in touch with your own and the collective unconscious. | You often feel misunderstood because no one experiences things as deeply as you do. |
| Your self boundaries are fluid so you can empathize with and understand others' experiences. | Your self boundaries become too permeable such that you take on others' feelings and lose touch with your own feelings and sense of yourself. |
| You are highly attuned to the feelings, moods, tone, and spirit of the group. | You can become overwhelmed by your feelings and those of others and not be able to detach and step back from them. |
| You are sensitive toward the fragile feelings of hurt, pain, loss, and grief. | You are prone to melancholy. You believe your suffering makes you special. |
| You have a sense for the drama and tragedy of life. | You can overreact and dramatize. Drama creates excitement, dispels boredom, and helps create a sense of being special. |
| You have a strong emotional resonance and responsiveness to life. | Your intense emotions may frighten others away. *"I feel, therefore I am."* |

| Positive Core Value Tendencies | Distorted Core Characteristics |
|---|---|
| You are romantic, poetic, nostalgic. | You may live in your romantic fantasies instead of in real life. |
| You feel fulfilled and whole in the present. | You focus on what is missing in the present; you can be nostalgic about paradise lost in the past and yearn for fulfillment in the future. |

## Objective Paradigm
*Originality*

**Adaptive Cognitive Schema:**

You are in touch with your real self and feel whole and complete. You believe you already are original.

You feel connected to yourself, to your roots and to the ground of your being. You feel at home.

## Distorting Paradigm
*Specialness*

**Maladaptive Cognitive Schema:**

You feel sad because you have become separated from your essential nature. You feel incomplete, inauthentic, lacking, and disoriented. You believe you must do something to make yourself special.

You feel abandoned, left behind. You see yourself as an aristocrat in exile, apart from the main. If you make yourself special, then maybe others will remember you and love you.

## Virtue: *Equanimity*

**Adaptive Emotional Schema:**

Right now you have everything you need to be perfectly happy. You appreciate yourself and your unique parcel of talents.

You express a balanced appropriate response to inner and outer stimuli.

## Passion: *Envy*

**Maladaptive Emotional Schema:**

You envy others who seem to have something you're missing. You envy others' relationships and happiness and naturalness.

You have exaggerated, dramatic mood swings.

## Area of Avoidance: *Ordinariness*

You fear the common and ordinary. If you're ordinary, you're nobody. The ordinary is boring and you want to be exciting. To exist you need to stand out from the crowd.

## Defense Mechanism: *Introjection*

Instead of simply grieving, letting go of the past, and getting on with your life, you carry your suffering and loss around inside of you. This melancholy is a familiar companion, and it makes you feel special. Yearning and longing are constantly in the background of your experience.

### How the Distortion of This Style Developed

- You originally felt close to a strong parent (often the father), then that parent went away (perhaps because your parent died, or your parents divorced, or the parent became busy at work, or a sibling was born, or the parent withdrew for some other emotional reason).

- You felt abandoned and interpreted that experience to mean there was something wrong with you or you weren't good enough—otherwise you wouldn't have been left behind.

- Then you tried to create yourself into a *special* person that the parent would notice and love. You came to believe that if you were special, then others would pay attention to you and wouldn't leave you.

- Your sense of tragedy, loss, and suffering may come from some original experience of being abandoned.
- Your mood swings may come from the alternation of a parent being available to you or not or of being kind or cruel. When the parent was there, you felt *good* about yourself and *up*. When the parent wasn't there, you felt *bad* about yourself and *down*.
- You felt expelled from the garden of love and are now longing to be readmitted.
- You received attention if you were sick or suffering; otherwise you weren't noticed.
- You got attention and your identity from living at the edges, at the extremes.
- You came to believe that being ordinary or calm meant being nobody or being boring.
- You felt alive especially when you made yourself *feel* intensely.
- Living intensely or living in your romantic world made you feel more special and important than living in the world as it is.
- You found you could compete successfully in the arena of style and flair.

**What You Miss as a Result of the Distortion of Your Style**
- The spontaneous expression of your thoughts and feelings.
- A balanced, modulated life style.
- Intimacy; being close to others without fear of rejection of being abandoned.

- The sense of fulfillment and satisfaction with who you are and what you have.
- The sense of being connected by your common humanity, being a part of the whole instead an island.
- Really having what you want vs. yearning for it.

## Paradigm Shifts You May Experience Under Stressful Conditions

*A Shift to the Low Side of Your Own Style*
- You may channel your feelings into your body and become physically ill instead of letting your feelings energize and guide your actions.
- Your mood swings may widen, with your lows becoming lower and your highs higher.
- Instead of being assertive and expressing your anger cleanly, you may become either passive-aggressive and suffer, complain and blame more, or you may become aggressive and vindictive and vengeful.
- As you feel worse about yourself or consider it's your fault that things aren't as you would like them, suicidal thoughts may preoccupy you more. Suicide may have several functions: it makes you special; it stops the suffering; it gets even with others; it lets them realize what they've done to you and how much they'll miss you.
- You may move away from people and isolate yourself more.

- You may throw yourself into work and become hyperactive to avoid dealing with your real issues.

### A Shift to the Low Side of Style 2

- You may avoid dealing with your own needs and wishes and attend more to others' needs. Instead of being sensitive toward yourself, you become sensitive toward others.
- You might flee into service instead of healing yourself.
- You may repress your feelings instead of expressing them directly.
- You may become more manipulative instead of asking directly for what you want or taking action to get what you want.
- Your issues around dependence and independence may become exaggerated. You might become more possessive or more aloof.
- You may say, *"What's the use. I'm beyond repair, so I'll help others."*
- You could become a suffering servant, a martyr, a sacrificial victim.

### A Shift to the High Side of Style 2

- You can genuinely care for and serve people and get out of your self-absorption.
- You can accurately empathize with others.
- You can move towards others as well as away from them.

## Paradigm Shifts You May Experience
## Under Relaxed Conditions

### A Shift to the High Side of Your Own Style

- You realize you are already *original.* You don't have to be eccentric or make yourself special. You search for and find the beloved within you vs. outside you.
- You can be spontaneous and let yourself go instead of being so composed.
- You can find the extraordinary in the ordinary.
- You accept your unique parcel of talents and don't compare yourself with others. You use your envy to help you locate and appreciate the values in others and to find those values in yourself.
- You pay attention to your real feelings vs. the exaggerated feelings that come from the excitement of your moods. You move from an addiction to romance and fantasy to action in real life.
- You stay in the here and now and realize that right now you have all you need to be happy.

### A Shift to the High Side of Style 1

- You take an action-oriented, problem-centered approach. You think about what you can do about the problem vs. bemoaning your fate. You switch from a passive victim stance to being an active agent. You don't just yearn there, you do something. Put your show on the road instead of over-rehearsing.

- You focus on one feeling at a time. What are you feeling now? And what do you want to do about it? You stay specific and resist generalizations and dramatizations. You stay with the facts.

- You maintain a sense of proportion, balance, equanimity. You don't exaggerate your response or heighten the stimuli. You do exactly what the situation requites. You do your work objectively.

- You can say, *"I am good"* or *"I'm good enough as I am"* instead of *"I'm not good enough."* You reown your own strength, goodness, and wholeness.

- You can get in touch with your anger, focus it, and use it to get what you want instead of turning your anger against yourself, feeling depressed, and believing you don't deserve or can't attain what you want. You ask directly for what you want and state your needs directly.

- You realize that *realistic* isn't necessarily philistinistic.

- You can commit yourself to being in the world even though it is flawed and unfulfilling. You contribute to something you believe in.

### A Shift to the Low Side of Style 1

- You may throw yourself into work and become hyperactive.

- You may get messianic about your fantasies and become emotionally overinvolved with your idealistic principles. "I *must* do my life's work!"

- You can become overly critical of your relationships.

# Style 5
## The Wise Person

### Positive Descriptors of Your Style

thoughtful

scholarly

reflective

truth-seeking

prudent

observant

witty

pithy

reasonable

logical

circumspect

clear

understanding

non-intrusive

philosophical

perceptive

cool

informed

analyzer/synthesizer

### Negative Descriptors of Your Style

operate alone

miserly

overly-detached

unfeeling

uncaring

avoid commitment

cold

heady

postpone action

contemptuous

reclusive

abstract

intellectual

uncommunicative

greedy

hidden

hoarder

vicarious experience

holding back

fear of feelings

| Positive Core Value Tendencies | Distorted Core Characteristics |
|---|---|
| You value and are attracted to *wisdom*, knowledge, understanding. For you, the *intellect* is a person's highest faculty. "*I think, therefore I am.*" | You can overidentify with the *idealized self-image* of being *wise* and *perceptive*. You live too much out of your head and forget you also have feelings and a body. |
| Your passions are of the mind. | You can be overly intellectual. You may be afraid of and out of touch with your feelings. |
| You are a seeker of truth. You want to discover what really is. | You can become overly analytical and skeptical. Your questioning can interfere with your acting. |
| You are a perceptive, insightful, original thinker. | You may be unwilling to consider others' perceptions and ideas. |
| You have the ability to objectively and dispassionately observe. | You may stay in the observer position on the sidelines and not participate in life. |
| You are good at abstracting, synthesizing, and integrating different points of view and disparate elements. | You may not make a decision or act until you have the certitude that you have all the facts. You want to know everything before you do anything. |
| You are a fair, nonjudgmental witness. | You may be unwilling to disclose your own position. |

| Positive Core Value Tendencies | Distorted Core Characteristics |
|---|---|
| You are a good listener. You are gentle, patient, and non-threatening. | You may not contribute much to conversations. You let others do all the talking. |
| You have the ability to get to the essence or heart of the matter. You can peer through extraneous details to get to basic structures. | You can reduce life to bare dry bones (X-ray pictures) and miss the juicy, meaty aspects of life. |
| You can communicate in clean, clear, concise statements about what the issue really is. | You can be stingy with your communications. You speak in epigrams or one-liners and are unwilling to elaborate on what you've said. |
| You have an appreciation for solitude. | You can be addicted to privacy. You have an exaggerated need for space and anonymity. |
| You are independent and resourceful. | You can be a loner who wants to do everything out of your own resources. |
| You are reserved, respectful, and non-intrusive. | You have overdeveloped the tendency to *move away from* people. And it's difficult for you to move forward with either affection or assertion. |

## Objective Paradigm
*Understanding/ Transparency*

**Adaptive Cognitive Schema:**

Your wisdom and understanding come from experience, participation, and involvement. You know with your body-feelings-mind.

You share your inner life to enrich the world. You freely give what you have freely received. You are generous with your self, feelings, ideas, and time.

## Distorting Paradigm
*Intellectualization/ Anonymity*

**Maladaptive Cognitive Schema:**

Your knowledge comes too exclusively through your perceptions and watching and intellect. You know through your head or vicarious experience.

You desire anonymity, to hide and observe. You want to see but not be seen.

## Virtue: *Detachment*

**Adaptive Emotional Schema:**

You possess the spirit of non-attachment. You take what you need and let the rest go.

You express a balanced appropriate response to inner and outer stimuli.

## Passion: *Avarice*

**Maladaptive Emotional Schema:**

You are greedy. To avoid an inner sense of emptiness or feel externally dependent on others, you fill yourself and store up in yourself information and materials.

You hoard information and hold onto what you have and know. You are stingy with your time, possessions, ideas, feelings, and self.

## Area of Avoidance: *Emptiness*

Since you repress your feelings and minimize your intimate interactions with others, you can experience a sense of inner emptiness. You may believe you have nothing to offer. You are searching for the meaning of life. You also fear being emptied by others and so withdraw and hold on tight.

## Defense Mechanism: *Isolation*

To avoid feeling empty, you isolate yourself in your head away from your feelings and people. You go to your thoughts where you feel full and comfortable. You also isolate or compartmentalize one time or period of your life from the next.

### How the Distortion of This Style Developed

- You may have experienced an early separation from your mother so an initial bonding with her didn't take place and you withdrew into yourself.
- You experienced your mother and/or father (and so the world) as being depriving and withholding. So you became depriving, too, both toward others and toward yourself.
- You may have experienced your parents as being too intrusive, so you withdrew to protect your boundaries.
- You may have felt overprotected, smothered, or engulfed, so you retreated into your mind or into books.

- You discovered that the best offense was a good defense.
- You found that being invisible was a good way to survive. It's hard to hit a target you can't see.
- You can't be blamed for what you never said. If people don't know what you're thinking, they can't criticize you.
- You didn't feel listened to, so you didn't speak unless you were sure people wanted to hear you.
- You were successful with academics and were rewarded for being studious.
- Your inner world became safer, more secure, more controllable and more interesting than the outer world.
- The expression of feelings—especially anger or any exuberant feelings—were not encouraged in your family.

## What You Miss as a Result of the Distortion of Your Style

- The delights of being a sensual, bodily person.
- The joy and fulfillment of giving.
- The meaning that comes from becoming involved and engaged with life.
- The deep satisfactions of intimate, mutual personal relationships.
- The fun and excitement of being in the game instead of keeping yourself on the sidelines.
- The experience of being a part of (vs. apart from) humanity; feeling connected, belonging.

- The experience of trust and cooperation instead of trying to do everything yourself.
- The energy and aliveness and power of your own emotions which are your allies, not your enemies.
- Self-confidence.

## Paradigm Shifts You May Experience Under Stressful Conditions

### A Shift to the Low Side of Your Own Style

- Instead of moving out to make contact with people, either through assertion or affection, you may withdraw further and fall more silent.
- You might feel more inadequate and think you are unable to influence the situation, so you may do nothing.
- You may repress your feelings more or channel them into fantasies instead of into behavior.
- You may *back up* more and move *up* into your control tower in your head instead of moving *down* to get grounded in your feelings and body and then moving *out* into interactions.
- Instead of expressing your needs and negotiating, you take your ball and bat and go home and refuse to play in the game, believing that the world is non-negotiable.
- You may hold in your anger and become cold—like dry ice. You may freeze people out instead of engaging with them or inviting them in.

- You may become contemptuous of others instead of interacting with them. You may become critical and cynical as ways of avoiding contact.
- You may unplug, disconnect, and feel more alienated and isolated.

### A *Shift to the Low Side of Style 7*

- You may get more into your head, intellectualize, systematize, and spiritualize to avoid taking action.
- You may turn to humor to lighten the situation and make it seem less important to avoid asserting yourself.
- You might let your fear of suffering or getting hurt prompt you to avoid them by retreating.
- You might get into planning what you'll do the next time instead of doing something this time.
- You might look for what is good in the situation so you won't have to voice your displeasure at what you don't like.
- You may give up on your ability to analyze and go in depth into the matter at hand. Instead you may distract yourself with superficial diversions or pursue many interests at once rather than completing any one. You might become flighty and undependable.

### A *Shift to the High Side of Style 7*

- Your imagination and visualizing capabilities may be enhanced.
- You can use your humor to help you move toward people and be more sociable and friendly.

- You are more spontaneous and use play as a way of taking the edge off social encounters.


## Paradigm Shifts You May Experience
## Under Relaxed Conditions

### A *Shift to the High Side of Your Own Style*

- You own your relational powers. You *move toward,* protect, enrich, and enlarge others instead of defending yourself from others or holding back from them.
- You empathize as well as analyze; you listen with your heart as well as your head. You apply your knowledge instead of keeping it to yourself.
- You get in touch with your feelings, especially hurt and anger. You let them energize and express your real self.
- You allow yourself to be transparent. You come out in the open instead of trying to be invisible. You let yourself be known and seen. You challenge and let go of your addiction to isolation and privacy.
- You can successfully challenge your fear of looking foolish and your fear of making a mistake. You don't let them stop you from doing what you want. You don't have to know everything before you choose and act.
- You can come to each person and situation empty, without preconceptions, categories, and structures. You are open to what is there and trust

your spontaneous response. You trust your inner
perceptions, intuitions, and feelings.

- You stay with your sense of emptiness instead of
trying to avoid it or fill it. You may discover it is
really a fertile void, a container that is always open
to the here and now.

### A Shift to the High Side of Style 8

- You are in touch with your personal power. You *can*
change and influence the situation. You do have
something to offer. You are in touch with your inner
authority and stand up for what you believe in. You
can say to yourself, *"I am powerful; I can do."*

- You can own your assertive powers. You can *move
against*. You can say what you want or don't want.
You can ask for what you need. You balance input
with output. You reach out vs. pull back.

- You consult your body, instincts, heart, and feelings
as well as your head. You are in touch with your
instinctual energy.

- You move "down and out" vs. "up and away": *down*
into your feelings and gut reactions and *out* into
action; instead of *up* into your thoughts and away
from the situation. You put yourself out in the
world.

- You use your power and assertion to establish and
maintain stronger boundaries. You can set limits
instead of retreating. You stay in the ring and don't
jump out at the first sign of pain or opposition.

*A Shift to the Low Side of Style 8*

- You may become aggressive instead of assertive. You may become mean and cruel and use your power to grasp, hold on and remain stingy instead of being magnanimous and generous.

- You may exaggerate your independence and isolation and become more anti-social.

- You may become vindictive with a dose of paranoid thinking.

# Style 6
## The Loyal Person

### Positive Core Value Tendencies

cautious

reliable

traditional

God-fearing

respectful

loyal

responsible

trustworthy

sensible

determined

prepared

conscientious

stabilizing

charming

prudent

honorable

tenacious

devil's advocate

authority conscious

### Negative Descriptors of Your Style

dogmatic

suspecting

rigid

uptight

catastrophizing

authoritarian

phobic/counterphobic

timid

assume worst

indecisive

wary

conservative

vigilante

rule-follower or challenger

anxious

status quo

worrier

uncertain

need for guidelines

security conscious

## Positive Core Value Tendencies

## Distorted Core Characteristics

You are attracted to and value *loyalty*. You honor your commitments.

You can overidentify with the *idealized self-image* of being *loyal* and *doing your duty*.

When you give your word, you keep it. If you say you'll do something, you do it.

You can become rigid and inflexible. It may be difficult for you to change or reconsider your loyalties.

You are faithful to relationships. You make a gracious host or hostess. You are protective of those in your care. You are loyal and dedicated to your cause and group.

You can polarize reality and your relationships into friend or foe, in or out, for me or against me. While you are accepting of those inside the fold, you can become a persecutor of those outside the fold.

You are able to foster, support, and parent others.

You can become overprotecting, smothering, and restricting.

You make a devoted follower or leader. You are responsible and can be counted on to do what you're told or what you promise.

You may become authoritarian or anti-authoritarian. Your faith and devotion may be given blindly or attached to the wrong ideal.

You have a balanced attitude toward external authority and you trust your own inner authority.

You can be either overly fearful and dependent on authorities or overly challenge them to test whether they deserve their authority and your allegiance.

| Positive Core Value Tendencies | Distorted Core Characteristics |
|---|---|
| You have respect for law and order. | You may exaggerate your appreciation for structure and order into a paranoid police state. |
| You have an appreciation for your heritage. You honor your past. | You can become ultraconservative. You may be fearful of and uncomfortable with anything new. |
| You are prudent and cautious. | You may be overly cautious and spread fear and alarm. *"Be careful or you'll get hurt."* |
| You have a sense of propriety. You are respectful and reverent towards others. | You can be stuffy, serious, and obsequious. You restrict your spontaneity. |
| You are cooperative. | You may be either excessively compliant or rebellious. |
| You are *semper fidelis*, always faithful and constant. | You can be super-orthodox and conservative. |
| You are *semper paratus*, always prepared and ready for a crisis. | You are wary, fearful, and worrisome. You have nothing to fear but fear itself. |
| You can be an adventurous explorer. | You may believe you need to prove yourself by your daring or your duty. |

## Objective Paradigm
*Faith*

### Adaptive Cognitive Schema:

You have faith in a balanced and trustworthy world. You believe the universe is out to do you good, not to do you in.

You believe you are already connected to, trusted by, and on the side of the ground of your being. You believe the force is with you.

You are in touch with your own essence, spirit, and authority and with others' genuine selves which puts you at ease.

## Distorting Paradigm
*Doubt/Dogma*

### Maladaptive Cognitive Schema:

You perceive the world as alien, hostile, threatening, and dangerous, and this gives rise to fear and suspicion in you.

You believe the force is against you, or at least is testing you to see whether you'll be faithful and acceptable. You automatically give your allegiance to authority or you doubt authority and yourself.

You are in touch with your own and others' inner judge and critic which makes you nervous and fearful.

## Virtue: *Courage*

**Adaptive Emotional Schema:**

Your strength comes from being in harmony with your inner self and with the objective laws of the universe.

You are naturally courageous when you need to be. You spontaneously respond well in crises.

You are motivated by your heart and what you genuinely believe in.

## Passion: *Fear*

**Maladaptive Emotional Schema:**

Fear puts you out of touch with your real self and the real world and so you need to create a substitute strength and bravado.

You may become *counter-phobic* by recklessly pushing through your fears and forcing yourself to do what you're afraid of, or *phobic* by dying a thousand deaths through your cowardice and worry.

You are driven by fear and doubt.

**Area of Avoidance:** *Deviance*
If you are fearful, you seek to be loyal and obedient, you consider any disobedience, rebelliousness, or following your own inner authority to be deviant, unlawful, and unacceptable.

If you are counter-fearful, you become rebellious and seek to challenge, evade, or escape from authority.

**Defense Mechanism:** *Projection*
You project onto others your own sense of disobedience and rebellion. *Other people* are trying to get away with things, and you need to monitor their activities and bring them in line with your authority's principles, or others are trying to trip you up and trap you.

### How the Distortion of This Style Developed

- Your parents may have been authoritarian. They laid down the rules and you had to follow them.
- You had to please your parents and do what you were told vs. paying attention to what you wanted or thought or felt.
- Your parents may have been overly protective. They had a fearful attitude toward life which you picked up.
- You learned that the world was a dangerous place to be guarded against.
- There may have been some family secret that needed to be kept inside the family. So boundaries were

established between inside and outside. Familial
bonds and loyalty arose against the outside world.

- You found security in being close to authority.
- You decided to rebel against authority as a way to
  survive since the people who were authorities in your
  life abused their authority and couldn't be trusted.
- You came to believe that if you kept the law, the law
  would keep you.
- You got approval for being responsible, obedient,
  and hardworking.
- You had to assume the role of an adult before you
  were ready. You became the family caretaker.
- You felt incompetent because you weren't ready for
  this adult role and so you began to doubt yourself.
- Or you experienced a parent as being incompetent,
  and so you began to doubt authority.

### What You Miss as a Result of the Distortion of Your Style

- A sense of inner security.
- Being able to do what you want vs. what you ought.
- A relaxed attitude toward yourself, others, life, and
  a higher power.
- A gracious approach to life.
- Being carefree.
- Being inner-directed instead of outer-directed.
- Trust in yourself and others.
- The freedom of the children of God: freedom from
  the law vs. enslavement and idolatry toward it; the
  law is for you and not vice versa.

## Paradigm Shifts You May Experience
## Under Stressful Conditions

### A *Shift to the Low Side of Your Own Style*
- You may become more indecisive and worrisome.
- As you become more fearful, you may worry more about whether you're brave enough to do what is required of you. You may believe you need to prove yourself even more.
- You may become more suspicious of others.
- You might become more dogmatic and set in your beliefs and become more intolerant of other points of view.
- You might trust your inner authority less.
- You may act out against authority, becoming more rebellious and belligerent.

### A *Shift to the Low Side of Style 3*
- Instead of relaxing, you may speed up and become busier.
- Instead of dealing with your inner issues, you might distract yourself with external matters and take on more projects.
- Not only might you run around in circles in your head by obsessing and worrying, but you may engage your gears and literally run around in circles in frantic activity to avoid dealing with your inner issues or to prove yourself and gain authority's or others' approval.
- You may try to substitute some external role for the inner security you're really seeking.

- You may start to deceive yourself and others about who you really are, what you really think and feel, and what you really want.
- You may want to avoid any semblance of rebellion or independent thought. And you may also begin to avoid any form of failure. As a result, your inner and outer freedom will become less and less.
- You may try to please authority and win them over by working hard, being faithful, doing what you're told, playing your part, etc.

### A Shift to the High Side of Style 3
- You get in touch with your capacity to take action. You feel better when you are in action.
- You connect with your own competence and mastery to become proactive vs. reactive.
- You can channel your energy into goals and concrete plans instead of into fears and worst-case scenarios. You focus on what you can do vs. on what might go wrong.

## Paradigm Shifts You May Experience
## Under Relaxed Conditions

### A Shift to the High Side of Your Own Style
- You trust your own instincts, viewpoints and inner authority. You become more autonomous vs. being dependent on others' opinions, especially authority's pronouncements. You are secure within yourself

instead of seeking security from outside yourself. You develop a realistic belief in yourself and your abilities. You can affirm yourself.

- You develop the courage to be. You accept responsibility for your choices and act bravely. You trust your inner compass and desires. You believe that what you really want is what God wants for you.

- You trust that others aren't trying to get away with something. You believe they're trying to do the best they can. You don't project hostile intentions onto others.

- You recognize that rules are there for your benefit. You don't have to be a slave to them. You now follow the spirit of the law vs. the letter.

- You realize you are already a part of the operation or organization. You are already in the game. So you don't have to prove yourself to get in, and you don't have to worry about being thrown out.

- You can consider the positive outcomes as well as the negative ones. Your old inclination was to consider what could go wrong and that stopped you from acting. You were your own worst enemy. Now you can think of what might go right to motivate yourself to act.

- You trust your instinctual ability to protect and preserve yourself and those you love. You realize that nothing can harm your essence. You can challenge your fears—are they realistic or mythical?

*A Shift to the High Side of Style 9*

- You practice self-soothing and calming. You can say to yourself, *"I am settled"* vs. *"I am upset."*

- You can be still and quiet. You realize the solution lies within you. You calm your waters and let the solution surface.

- Instead of making mountains out of molehills, you make molehills out of mountains. You can say, *"What's the big deal"* instead of making a big deal out of everything.

- You have the relaxed mind set, *"So what if I do this or think that"* vs. the fearful and indecisive mind set of *"What if I do this or that?"* You can go with the flow and trust the process.

- You can relax and float and let the stream support you. You realize that struggling is not the solution.

- You can find the truth in all sides of an issue instead of polarizing the issue and making one side all true and the other side all false.

*A Shift to the Low Side of Style 9*

- You may become even more doubtful, ruminating, and indecisive.

- You may find yourself procrastinating and doing unimportant things to distract yourself from doing what you really need to do. You may find it hard to prioritize and discern what you really want.

- You may numb yourself out or put yourself into some routine to avoid anxiety-provoking situations.

# Style 7
## The Joyful Person

## Positive Descriptors of Your Style

lighthearted
optimistic
friendly
enthusiastic
creative
visionary
gregarious
imaginative
joyful
merrymaking

extroverted
excitable
appreciative
fun-loving
funny
entertaining
lively
planning
bright
spontaneous

## Negative Descriptors of Your Style

superficial
loquacious
narcissistic
cosmic
spacey
distracted
indulgent
light-headed
impulsive
irresponsible

inconsistent
unreliable
daydreamer
spotlight-grabbing
sybaritic
scattered
unrealistic
escapist
naive
dabbler

| Positive Core Value Tendencies | Distorted Core Characteristics |
|---|---|
| For you the purpose of life is to *enjoy* it. You value *joy*. There is a delight sparkle, and *joie de vivre* about you. | You can overidentify with the *idealized self-image* of being *okay*. You can overdo the pleasure principle and become overly attached to pleasure. |
| You are a celebrator of life. | You can become addicted to highs. |
| You have a great appreciation for life. Everything is recognized as gift. | You may not be willing to endure hard labor to get what you want. |
| You have a childlike responsiveness to the world. You are in touch with the immediacy of things. | You may be unwilling to follow up your initial enthusiasm with the boring work necessary to realize the project. The seed sprang up immediately but withered away because it didn't put down roots. |
| You are an advocate of growth, hope, and resurrection now. | You may trust only excitement, fireworks, consolation, and joy, and forget that growth also takes place in cold, dark silence. |
| You have an optimistic outlook on life. You can find the silver lining in black clouds. *"Two prisoners looked out from prison bars; one saw mud, the other saw stars."* | Your computer is set on *nice* and nothing is allowed in that is not nice. You can be a compulsive optimist seeing the world through rose-colored glasses. |

## Positive Core Value Tendencies

## Distorted Core Characteristics

You have a creative imagination and are a wellspring of new ideas.

You may confuse your map and plan with reality and action.

You are lively, vivacious, and colorful.

You may be unwilling to look at the dark side of pain and suffering.

You are friendly and gregarious and are good at cheering people up.

Your relationships may remain superficial. *"Hale fellow well met."*

You are a natural entertainer and storyteller.

You may live your stories instead of your life.

You are a visionary, a long-range planner.

You can get into head trips instead of doing serious work.

You can generate endless possibilities. You are an intuitive person.

You can become a dilettante and jump from one interest to another without digesting anything thoroughly or without completing any project.

## Objective Paradigm
*Work*

**Adaptive Cognitive Schema:**

When you are living in touch with your real self, then you are also living in accordance with the cosmic plan or the divine scheme of things. You understand that each person has a part to play in the evolution of humankind.

Work can be play when you do what you love doing.

## Distorting Paradigm
*Pleasure/Planning*

**Maladaptive Cognitive Schema:**

When you lose touch with your real self and live out of your personality, then you are not participating in the larger scheme of things. You substitute your own plans and search for pleasure in place of deeper satisfactions.

If it isn't fun, it isn't worth doing and you don't stay with it for long.

## Virtue: *Sobriety*

**Adaptive Emotional Schema:**

Sobriety means living in the present and living a balanced life, taking in only as much as you need and expending only as much energy as is called for.

## Passion: *Gluttony*

**Maladaptive Emotional Schema:**

Gluttony means overindulgence, planning future fun-filled events, and spicing up life with excitement and fluff.

**Area of Avoidance:** *Pain and Suffering*

Since you want to appear happy and okay you are uncomfortable with and find unacceptable any form of pain. You may either be out of touch with the pain in your life, or you are aware of it but are unwilling to show it to others since your job is to cheer people up, not weigh them down with your problems.

**Defense Mechanism:** *Sublimation*

To keep pain out of your awareness, you sublimate it and turn it into something interesting or good. You automatically look for the good in everything. So you might celebrate the new life of a deceased loved one rather than mourn their loss.

### How the Distortion of This Style Developed

- You found that a cheerful, pleasant disposition earned approval from others and got you what you needed.
- You learned that your smiles elicited smiles from others.
- You were rewarded for cheering up the family, not complaining, and for keeping things light.
- Entertaining others and being the life of the party got you attention.
- People may have listened to your stories more than to your real self, or they were more interested in your stories than in your hurt or pain.

- You got more enjoyment from planning projects than from executing them.
- Your childhood was basically a happy one, or at least you turned it into being happy or you remember it as being happy.
- Even if you experienced adversity in your childhood, you learned to laugh about it to survive.
- You may have been shielded from hurt and pain or didn't experience much of either. And so you didn't learn how to deal with them—except by avoiding them.
- You may have learned that what you don't see won't hurt you.

**What You Miss as a Result of the Distortion of Your Style**

- A sense of inner strength and satisfaction that comes from working hard at something and accomplishing it.
- A deep character that is etched by perseverance and suffering and endurance.
- Experiencing the full range of emotions, the negative as well as the positive.
- Meeting your *Shadow* and discovering its riches.
- The tranquility of solitude, silence, and inner stillness.
- The experience of growth in desolation.
- Not being afraid of the dark.
- Thoroughly understanding something.
- Deep interpersonal relationships based on sharing all of yourself, not just the bright or light sides.

## Paradigm Shifts You May Experience
## Under Stressful Conditions

*A Shift to the Low Side of Your Own Style*
- You may get more into your head. You may intellectualize, spiritualize, and sublimate more.
- You may get more into planning and further away from doing. You may avoid doing hard work in favor of making future plans.
- You might try to avoid the present pain by imagining future or past pleasures.
- You may attempt to lighten things up even more, laugh off the situation, and not take yourself seriously.
- You may continue attempting to outrun your fears by looking for more parades to lead or join.

*A Shift to the Low Side of Style 1*
- You may become angry and resentful that your life is not as enjoyable as you would like it to be. Your joyful expectations are not being met.
- You may express your anger through sarcastic wit or critical remarks or through resentment and believing that life isn't fair—or at least not fun enough.
- You may complain and blame others for raining on your parade, spoiling your fun, popping your balloons. Others are keeping you from realizing all your fantastic schemes.
- You may give up on your natural appreciation for life and your spontaneous ability to find good in

everything and begin to become critical and caustic toward yourself and others. You begin to notice what is missing instead of what is there.

- If you get too critical or too disappointed, you may become depressed.
- You may swing from being optimistic to being pessimistic, but probably not for long.
- You may give up trying to look okay. You may stop smiling.
- You may avoid and deny your anger as well as avoiding pain and suffering.

### A Shift to the High Side of Style 1

- You can become more disciplined and focused and follow through on your plans and projects, bringing them to completion.
- Instead of doing what is pleasurable, you can be motivated by what is the right thing to do or what is called for.
- You take a more objective delineated point of view in place of a fantastic impressionistic vision.
- You attend to details and sweat the small stuff vs. going cosmic with global impressions.

## Paradigm Shifts You May Experience
## Under Relaxed Conditions

*A Shift to the High Side of Your Own Style*

- You can be present to all that is there: the good *and* the bad, the pleasurable *and* the painful, the light *and* the dark, the yin and the yang. Truth involves honoring both polarities.

- You can be sober. You aren't afraid to take yourself and the situation seriously. Even if you do get heavy, you know you won't crash.

- You trust that if you let go of your wings and balloons, you won't fall into the tomb. And even if you do, you believe that desolation and darkness can be growth-producing.

- You do what is worth doing. You realize happiness is contingent upon your doing your share of social and personal work.

- You can stay in the here and now and resist projecting yourself into the future. You do what you're doing instead of making future plans.

- You believe that your insights are important enough to work towards actualizing them.

- You stay with the pain instead of trying to avoid it, rationalize it, sublimate it, etc.

- Instead of making light of a situation, you can express your anger or be assertive.

*A Shift to the High Side of Style 5*

- You can say to yourself, *"I am wise and perceptive"* vs. *"I am a lightweight or scatterbrained."*
- You can channel your energies and stay focused instead of scattering and getting distracted.
- You stay with what you're doing and thoroughly investigate it until you really understand it.
- You chew and digest instead of gulping down indiscriminately.
- You put your creative bursts and intuitions into some system and structure. You are thorough and methodical. This helps you take the next step of action.
- You learn to appreciate silence and aloneness.
- You can be still and observant. You can take the position of the fair witness, the detached observer.
- You watch vs. react. You develop your interiority.
- You practice detachment. You can move back a little from what's going on instead of losing yourself in what's happening.

*A Shift to the Low Side of Style 5*

- You may withdraw and try to disappear.
- You may compound your gluttonous life style with being avaricious and desirous of accumulating even more possessions and experiences.
- You might become more unhinged from reality and more glued to your fantasies and ideas.

# Style 8
## The Powerful Person

**Positive Descriptors of Your Style**

forceful

strong

direct

assertive

own person

autonomous

influential

hardworking

high energy

confident

magnanimous

strong-willed

no nonsense

take lead

fair

just

honorable

fearless

assured

competent

**Negative Descriptors of Your Style**

vengeful

unrefined

macho

bravuro

get even

possessive

overwhelming

intimidating

loud

gruff

bully

insensitive

non-listening

calloused

tough

domineering

belligerent

dictatorial

chip-on-shoulder

confrontive

| Positive Core Value Tendencies | Distorted Core Characteristics |
|---|---|
| You are attracted to and appreciate *power*. You know how to get it, keep it, and use it. | You can overidentify with the *idealized self-image* of being *powerful* and *capable*. You can become addicted to power and control and rely on it to manipulate others. |
| You use your influence to bring about good. | You use your power to protect yourself instead of to help others. |
| You make a strong leader like a matriarch or a patriarch. | You can become a dictator, bully, godfather or godmother. |
| You are self-confident, self-assured and have a healthy self-image. | Your presence can be overbearing and intimidating. |
| You are independent and autonomous. You value being your own person. | You can exhibit an exaggerated independence and take pride in doing your own thing. |
| You can be magnanimous and use your personal power to contribute to and build up the community. | You can be self-aggrandizing and use your power against the community. |
| You have the ability to inspire others to accomplish great things. | You can coerce others by making them an offer they can't refuse. You influence by intimidation. |

| Positive Core Value Tendencies | Distorted Core Characteristics |
|---|---|
| You are direct, straightforward, honest, and tell it like it is. | You can be overly blunt and crude. |
| You can be a charismatic and inspiring person. | You can be insensitive to others' defenses and vulnerabilities in your unmasking of their pretensions. |
| You are able to cut through phoniness and fluff to get to the real issue. You believe in "no bullshit." | You may run roughshod over others or alienate them by taking over. |
| You are energized by challenge. You can take charge in difficult situations. | You can be aggressive. You get heard because you yell the loudest. |
| You are assertive and know-how to get what you want. | You are often the topdog and can oppress others. |
| You have a concern for the underdog and will fight on his/her behalf. | You can intimidate and mesmerize others into following you. |
| You do everything with gusto, enthusiasm, and great energy. | You can be driven and use up people and things in your path. |

## Objective Paradigm
### *Justice*

**Adaptive Cognitive Schema:**

You have an appreciation for justice and equity. You believe in the equal distribution of power.

You trust the fairness of the universe. You believe that what goes around, comes around, *"Vengeance is mine, saith the Lord."*

## Distorting Paradigm
### *Vindication*

**Maladaptive Cognitive Schema:**

You believe in "an eye for an eye and a tooth for a tooth." Justice becomes vengeance, getting even to maintain the balance of power.

You judge that what is happening isn't fair. So you need to create your own truth and take justice into your own hands. *"Vengeance is mine, saith the Eight."*

## Virtue: *Innocence*

**Adaptive Emotional Schema:**

You possess a childlike innocence. You are capable of experiencing each moment fresh without expectations and prejudgments.

Innocence means not harming. You have the attitude, *"Why should I want to harm anyone and why would anyone want to harm me?"*

You are satisfied with life as it is.

## Passion: *Lust*

**Maladaptive Emotional Schema:**

You come to each situation jaded, expecting trouble, or to be taken advantage of. You are therefore ready for a fight.

You have experienced aggression towards you in the past. So you want to get them before they get you.

You are lustful, meaning you do everything to *excess*. You can be possessive, grabby, and demanding.

## Area of Avoidance: *Weakness*

Since you want to appear strong, you must avoid any semblance of weakness. You are out of touch with your feminine side. You avoid tenderness, compassion, kindness, etc. as unbefitting a powerful person.

## Defense Mechanism: *Denial*

To prevent weakness from showing up in your awareness or persona, you deny any presence of it. *"I don't hurt, I'm not nice, I'm not sentimental, I don't need you,"* etc.

### How the Distortion of This Style Developed

- You may have been abused as a child and so became tough and aggressive in order to protect yourself.
- You may have witnessed considerable fighting and aggression in your family.
- You had to grow up fast and be hard to take care of yourself.
- You learned that when you challenged others or bullied them, you got your way.
- You were instructed to fight back and not put up with insults or injustices.
- You may have learned that in your family you don't get mad, you get even.
- You may have felt yourself to be a victim of injustice, so you grew up blaming the world.
- You learned never to give a sucker an even break.

- You learned never to show weakness if you wanted to survive.
- Since the world seemed to be arbitrary or unjust, you learned to make and follow your own rules.
- You realized you had a lot of energy and forcefulness. You had the ability to take charge, and you enjoyed being powerful.
- If a situation seemed threatening or falling apart, you felt more secure when you took control.

**What You Miss as a Result of the Distortion of Your Style**

- Being comforted by others and being touched by their care.
- Having someone speak up for you.
- Experiencing your own tenderness and softness and gentleness.
- Forgiveness and compassion.
- Being able to live with weakness instead of always having to deny it.
- The experience of reverence and respect for creatures instead of using them up.
- Letting your guard down and being vulnerable.
- The capacity to relax, to be present.
- Experiencing others' goodness and goodwill instead of anticipating their affronts.

## Paradigm Shifts You May Experience
## Under Stressful Conditions

### A *Shift to the Low Side of Your Own Style*

- You might try to take care of yourself by becoming more aggressive and tough. You send your anger out first to cover the hurt or sadness or disappointment you may really be feeling.
- You may become more intense, grabby, lustful, and possessive to fill up feeling empty inside.
- You may attempt to take more control and assume more power to feel secure.

### A *Shift to the Low Side of Style 5*

- You may give up on your own power and withdraw. You may *move away from* people instead of *toward* them.
- You may become quiet and want to be by yourself. You may isolate yourself from others.
- You may turn your power against yourself and beat up on yourself for your perceived weaknesses and injustices.
- Instead of exploding, you *implode* your energy and suck it inside yourself.
- As a result of imploding, you might experience exaggerated feelings of deadness and emptiness.
- You may drive yourself into a black hole. Then you may either become suicidal or become more desperate in your attempts to avoid this inner emptiness through living intensely.

- You may break contact with others vs. making contact.
- You won't let others support you or comfort you.
- You may exaggerate being independent and on your own. You become the Lone Ranger or Rangerette.
- You might become overly heady and rational and use your intellect to defend yourself, blame others, or plot revenge.
- You may feel inadequate and unable to influence the situation.
- You may begin to distrust your instincts.
- You might move toward thinking and observing instead of doing.

### A *Shift to the High Side of Style 5*

- You think before you act. You can think it out before you impulsively act it out.
- You can think clearly and dispassionately vs. with prejudiced preconceptions and caricatures.
- You connect your head and gut and heart and are genuinely present, spontaneous and compassionate vs. being internally disconnected and then feeling isolated, violent, or punishing.
- You appreciate and pursue knowledge for its own sake vs. as a way of having power over others.

## Paradigm Shifts You May Experience
## Under Relaxed Conditions

*A Shift to the High Side of Your Own Style*

- You let others speak up for you instead of always speaking up for them.
- You can share your vulnerable underside with others. You let them know your scared little kid. You let others support you.
- You move towards *interdependence* in place of your extreme self-sufficiency and fear of dependence.
- You trust others' motivations instead of challenging them and attempting to unmask their hidden motivations and intentions.
- You respect others' rights as much as you demand respect for your own.
- You speak the truth in a way that others can take it in instead of shoving it down their throat.
- You assume an attitude of innocence: why would anyone want to hurt you? And why would you want to hurt anyone?
- You come to each moment and situation fresh, without expectation of being hurt or taken advantage of and without memories of past wrongs and insults. You come with hands open vs. fists clenched.
- You trust that justice and fairness will come about without your intervention or having to get even. You realize it is not solely up to you to bring about justice and equity.

### A *Shift to the High Side of Style 2*

- You can be compassionate toward yourself and others. You temper your justice with mercy.
- You can say, *"I am helpful; I am giving."* You are giving instead of grabby.
- You use your power to build others up and empower them vs. tearing them down.
- You are empathic and sensitive toward your own needs and towards others' needs and feelings.
- You are in touch with your gentle side and tenderness. There is nothing stronger than true gentleness and nothing gentler than true strength. You become soft vs. hard—tender vs. tough.
- You move *toward* others vs. *against* them. You resist moving toward violence or vengeance.

### A *Shift to the Low Side of Style 2*

- You may engage in enabling behavior to make people dependent on you so they will affirm your strength.
- You may manipulate or intimidate others into needing your services in the manner of the Mafia to buttress your own position.
- You use your Godfather or Godmother position for your own aggrandizement vs. for the good of the community.

# Style 9
## The Peaceful Person

### Positive Descriptors of Your Style

patient

unostentatious

diplomatic

low key

reassuring

modest

objective

unflappable

settled

comfortable

receptive

allowing

permissive

peaceful

in harmony

calm

*laissez-faire*

easy going

down to earth

few expectations

### Negative Descriptors of Your Style

put things off

confluent

indecisive

low energy

distractible

squelch anger

boring

tedious

uncommitted

neglectful

overly adaptable

indolent

passive-aggressive

detached

unresponsive

oblivious

appeasing

unreflective

obstinate

difficulty discriminating

## Positive Core Value Tendencies

## Distorted Core Characteristics

You value *peace* which is the tranquility of order.

You can over-identify with the *idealized self-image* of being being *settled* and avoid any kind of conflict.

You have an intuitive sense and appreciation for harmony, for when things fit together.

You can overdo agreement. You experience ambivalence about whether to agree or disagree, to conform or not conform.

You possess diplomacy. You are able to reconcile opposing forces and can see both sides of an issue.

You may have difficulty taking a position or choosing sides. You can be indecisive or put off making any decision.

You have an allowing, *laissez-faire* approach to life which encourages people and events to unfold in their own way and at their own pace.

You can assume a passive stance towards life and take the path of least resistance. You can be unassertive and unwilling to intervene on your own behalf. You let things go too long unattended.

You are easygoing and give others freedom and space and let them take the lead.

You can get caught in the dilemma of fearing to express yourself lest you displease others and risk their abandoning you or of feeling resentful because you abandoned yourself and didn't get your needs met.

| Positive Core Value Tendencies | Distorted Core Characteristics |
|---|---|
| You have a calming, reassuring presence. | You may fiddle while Rome burns and refuse to recognize real problems. |
| You are a non-judgmental, accepting, impartial, and open listener. | You identify so much with others' positions that you may lose touch with or not express your own opinions and preferences. |
| You can be aware of and attentive to the nuances of each moment. | You have a tendency to generalize, homogenize, and not recognize differences. |
| You can be in tune with your personal preferences and feelings. | You pay attention to others' feelings but not your own. You can repress and numb out your anger and express it in a passive-aggressive manner. |
| You have a sense of purpose. | You sometimes believe you don't matter or make a difference. |
| You are a salt of the earth, down to earth, modest, unassuming person. You are even-tempered and have no need to show off. | You may lack a sense of self-worth and so don't take care of yourself physically, emotionally, socially, intellectually, or spiritually. |

## Objective Paradigm
*Love*

---

**Adaptive Cognitive Schema:**

You have a sense that you are loved, that you are lovable, and that you are capable of loving.

You are genuinely content with yourself and with reality as it is.

## Virtue: *Action*

---

**Adaptive Emotional Schema:**

Love wants to pass itself on through action. Gratitude for being loved leads to spontaneous action towards the welfare of the beloved. Action is natural to the real self and works for the development of that self.

When you are in touch with your real self, you know what you need and want and you know what you need to do to get what you want.

The integration of your feelings and thoughts motivate and focus your activity.

## Distorting Paradigm
*Resignation*

---

**Maladaptive Cognitive Schema:**

You feel deprived of love and not paid attention to, so you resign yourself, don't let yourself feel or want much, don't let things get to you, and don't make a big deal out of anything.

You can resign yourself to accepting whatever comes your way.

## Passion: *Indolence*

---

**Maladaptive Emotional Schema:**

Self-doubt and resignation lead to indolence or laziness regarding the growth of oneself and others. Procrastination, indecision, confusion, and inaction arise from the false personality and block action.

When you are inattentive to and neglectful of yourself, you don't know what you need, and so you don't act.

You can distract yourself and diffuse your activity when it comes to doing something really important to you.

**Area of Avoidance:** *Conflict*
Because you want to be settled, you avoid conflict or anything that would upset you. You pull for agreement and blur differences. You pour oil on troubled waters. You don't hear the squeaks since you want everything to go smoothly.

**Defense Mechanism:** *Narcotidzation*
To avoid conflict you numb your feelings, wants, and preferences. You make everything the same and highlight nothing. You make molehills out of mountains.

### How the Distortion of This Style Developed

- You weren't paid attention to enough when you were growing up. You felt neglected and then you neglected yourself.
- Instead of coming to the painful acknowledgement that you weren't loved or cared for or that you apparently didn't matter, you took a less painful stance of resignation by saying, *"It doesn't matter. What's the difference. Why make a big deal out of anything. Life is short."*
- You turned down your energy, lowered your expectations, and became resigned for the duration.
- You may have grown up in the background, felt overlooked, or overshadowed by your siblings.
- You weren't listened to and so you learned not to listen to yourself. You learned not to pay attention

to yourself, your needs, your preferences and wants, your feelings.

- You were caught in the dilemma of confronting others and being abandoned or of conforming to others and being controlled.

- So you took both sides instead of choosing sides. You developed indecision as a conflict-resolution method.

- You experienced a conflict between being good or bad, conformist or non-conformist, agreeing or disagreeing.

- Your solution was not to decide. You learned to postpone, to wait and see, to allow events to take their own course.

- You learned to comfort yourself by setting up a routine and going on automatic pilot.

- Your attempts to express your anger did not meet with success, so you repressed it.


**What You Miss as a Result of the Distortion of Your Style**

- A sense of accomplishment in getting things done.
- A sense of competency and self efficacy: *"I can do it."*
- Feeling loved and cared for and in turn being loving and caring.
- A sense of self-worth: *"I really do matter."*
- A sense of aliveness and vitality.
- The excitement and growth that arise out of conflict.
- A sense of purpose and destiny; you have a place in and a part to play in die unfolding of the universe.

## Paradigm Shifts You May Experience
## Under Stressful Conditions

### A Shift to the Low Side of Your Own Style

- You might say, *"What's the use?"* and become more resigned, more shut down.
- You may avoid confrontation and conflict.
- You may fall asleep, not notice, and not listen instead of dealing with the problem.
- You may become obstinate and unyielding.
- You might avoid even more not taking a position or stating your case.
- Instead of getting organized, you might become more disorganized and therefore unable to act.
- You may procrastinate, put off, and delay more.
- You may become more dependent on others to take care of you.
- You may become overly preoccupied with details and not finish what really needs to get done.
- You might distract yourself by pursuing unimportant, inconsequential matters instead of doing what you need to do.
- You may find yourself sleeping more or daydreaming more.

### A Shift to the Low Side of Style 6

- You may become worrisome, fearful, ruminative.
- You may begin to say, *"What if?"* instead of your usual *"So what if?"*
- You may begin making mountains out of molehills.

- You may doubt yourself and your own inner authority and avoid expressing your needs and your position.
- You might begin seeking the approval and affirmation and protection of some outside authority.
- You may become overly responsible and dutiful.
- You could become scrupulous and be overly concerned about keeping the rules and schedule.
- You may stop being relaxed and become rigid and obsessive.

### A *Shift to the High Side of Style 6*

- You can find in yourself the courage to be somebody and take a stand and state your case.
- You can push through your fears of being rejected or ignored, discover what you really want to do and act on those personal desires and preferences.

### Paradigm Shifts You May Experience Under Relaxed Conditions

### A *Shift to the High Side of Your Own Style*

- You can focus and differentiate instead of distracting yourself and becoming confluent.
- You are prompt. You do it now instead of procrastinating.
- You can be assertive. You state your own position, feeling, or preference. You are in touch with your

anger and use it to tell you what you want and to enable you to get what you really need.

- You trust your inner authority and resist turning to gurus or other external sources for energy and solutions.
- You are mindful of when you have been loved and touched and cared for. You allow your natural gratitude to lead you to action.
- You are awake to your real self, feelings, and wants. You resist falling asleep and neglecting yourself. You practice mindfulness. You remember yourself vs. being in a trance and forgetting who you are and what you want.
- You take better care of your inner spiritual well-being and your outer physical well-being.
- You don't substitute inconsequentials and nonessentials for what you really need and want.

### A *Shift to the High Side of Style 3*

- You can get focused and goal-oriented. You determine what you want and go get it in a step-by-step manner.
- You become organized and structured from within so you don't have to rely on external pressure to get you moving.
- You aren't just there, you do something. You take action to affect the world. You are in touch with your efficacious self, in touch with the active agent in you instead of being a passive recipient.

- You generate your own energy vs. draining off others' energy.
- You think of yourself as being professional, efficient, and competent.
- You can say to yourself: *"I am successful."*
- You assume the attitude that you are important, you do matter and make a difference instead of your usual *"It doesn't matter"* or *"I don't matter."*

### A Shift to the Low Side of Style 3

- You may engage in busy work as another way to distract yourself or neglect what you really need to work on.
- You may take on many projects to have something to do instead of intentionally living your own life.
- You may assume a role or some corporate identity and still not know who you are.

# Appendix
## Subtypes

## Style One: The Good Person

### Self preservation subtype

When anger leaks into and contaminates the instinct for preserving life, the result is the state of **anxiety** and **worry**. Anger gets acted out through agitation. Self preservation ONES worry about their survival and their health. They fear not being perfect or making mistakes which might imperil their survival. If they're not perfect, other people won't like them, will criticize them, and will eventually reject them.

Their own inner critic can be quite dominant. This angry voice scares them and leaves them feeling anxious. Their inner censor also frequently interrupts the ONES' speech and train of thought by proposing objections, addendum's, clarifications, etc.

The anger and resentment of self preservation ONES frequently gathers around issues of fairness and justice.

For example, they may decry the unfairness of their having to work so hard and overcome so many obstacles while things come so easily to their less-deserving neighbors.

Self preservation ONES can be confused with Phobic SIXES who are also fearful and worry about what can go wrong. ONES are more concerned about not coming up to the standards of their *internal* canons of perfection while SIXES are fearful about transgressing some *external* rule or code of authority. They might also be confused with self-preservation THREES who are trying to be good and perfect models.

**Social subtype**

When anger contaminates the instinct for belonging and social/group relations, **non-adaptability** is the result. Here anger gets expressed through rigid uncompromising social ideals and beliefs. Though Social ONES are more easygoing and express their energy more moderately than the intense Intimate ONES, they can become stubborn and refuse to budge on certain issues, often in the area of morality. They come across as very moralizing, insisting that things be done their way, taking a stand on their moral code because they believe they are in the right. They, too, are often social reformers who want to change the system rather than conform to society's code of ethics. They have difficulty identifying with or going along with the system if they believe it is not morally correct. For example, Abraham Lincoln wanted a united nation but risked a schism because he would not accommodate to the prevailing morality that sanctioned slavery.

Social ONES may form a group to get people to adopt their point of view, or join a group of like-minded people such as "Birthright" or "Freedom of Choice." ONES find themselves fully convicted on either side of controversies.

Social ONES can occasionally look like FIVES when they set themselves apart from their less than perfect peers.

### Intimate subtype

The word that characterizes this subtype's mental preoccupation, emotional vice, and reactive behavior is **jealousy**. When the vice of anger contaminates the natural drive for connection, intimate relationships, and sexual expression, the result is the experience of jealousy. The ego's anger gets channeled into jealousy which then becomes the personality's driving force and compelling issue. ONES are concerned that someone more perfect than they are will come along and draw away their partner or friend. They can become hyper judgmental of anyone or anything that might come between them and their mate. Others are seen as rivals who must be competed with and defended against.

This jealousy can also be expressed as being jealous for the cause or jealous for the rights of others. In this scenario jealousy becomes zealotry. And the word that describes this state is **zeal**. ONES can become intense and heated about the causes and persons they have espoused. Intimate ONES appear very righteous and devoted and are often crusaders and social reformers.

The intimate subtype is usually the clearest expression of exaggerated ONE energy. They are going to move into your space and make you better whether you asked for it or not. They are going to correct you, shape you up, and make you a decent human being even if it kills them, or you, in the process. This subtype drives their children to ballet, etiquette, gymnastic classes, etc.—for the child's own good. It is also the spouse that takes the partner off to a marriage counselor or to a communications workshop—for the betterment of the relationship.

This is the *countertype*. Whereas other ONES tend to be more puritanical and anti-instinctual, the anger of intimate ONES can fuel their desires and give them a righteous sense of entitlement to do what they deem best. They can sometimes be mistaken for the intimate subtype EIGHT.

## Style Two: The Loving Person

### Self preservation subtype

When pride intermingles with the instinct for self preservation, the result is the expectation of **privilege**. This is the "me first" attitude. This sense of entitlement or self-importance might seem contradictory and out of place in humble TWOS who profess to put others first. That's why this is the *countertype*. The spirit here is that they deserve to be first in our life because of all that they've done for us. They deserve to be esteemed and cared for because they've given so much of themselves away. Their sacrifices and contributions demand retributions.

This is a pride of place. Because of their "saintly" behavior and demeanor and because they have helped others succeed, they are entitled to first place—or, at least, preferential treatment. As they show their importance by being the first to help out, we cannot help but applaud and approve of them and invite them to the front of the line.

The variation on the theme of recognition and acceptance here is that Self preservation TWOS want to be central in some individual's life, in contrast to Social TWOS who additionally want to be the center of a group's attention.

Self preservation TWOS are more anxious, timid and shy than the other subtype manifestations. Hard working, loyal assistants (the power behind the throne) are frequently Self preservation TWOS. They can be confused with hard working, loyal assistant SIXES. Whereas fear and security are more lively issues for the SIXES, image and attention are of greater concern to the TWOS.

They might also look like FOURS in their longing for love.

While Intimate TWOS may use their sexuality to entice or coerce sexual involvement to prove that they are loved, Self preservation TWOS appear more innocent and childlike and seek affectionate affirmation more than sexual validation. Self preservation TWOS can look "cute" and not-so-adult; Social TWOS look over-adult; and intimate TWOS appear like a seductive adult.

## Social subtype

When pride combines with and contaminates the instinct for social relations, **ambition** is the result. The original meaning of ambition was to go around soliciting votes. For Social TWOS it means going around soliciting the attention and approval of the public. They are concerned about their status and image in the group. Pride distorts the TWOS' genuine humanitarian interest.

Social TWOS want to be close to and be seen with (not necessarily go to bed with) people who have power and prestige. They want to be important to others and especially important to "power persons."

The pride here is that they are someone because they are vitally needed. And they are all the more important because they are needed by important people. In their desire to be noticed by and be seen with prestigious people, TWOS can overlook those who don't have sufficient status to bolster their ego. So, ironically, their compulsion may miss those who are most needy.

Social TWOS may also be ambitious to be on the throne. They might set up service organizations, expecting to be admired and paid attention to for their helpful endeavors. They deserve to be the center of the group's attention because they are so wonderful and generous. They confuse being noticed and admired with being loved.

Social TWOS might appear like Social EIGHTS or THREES because they get things done and aspire to positions of influence and status.

If TWOS don't pursue their own ambitions, they might hitch their wagon to other stars, living out their ambitions through their spouses, children, employees, students, etc.

As with the other Social subtypes, the energy of Social TWOS is more moderate than the more intense energy of Intimate TWOS. They tend to be less aggressive, direct, and obvious in their attempts to involve others in their interpersonal style.

**Intimate subtype**
When the passion of pride leaks into and contaminates the pure expression of sexuality and the drive for connection, the compensating motivation or driving force becomes **sexual seduction** in its feminine archetype and **sexual aggression** as its masculine manifestation. Both maneuvers, which can be employed by either men or women, express a strong desire for connection and relationship.

*Seduction* stems from the TWOS' maladaptive schema that believes their worth comes from feeling accepted and loved from the outside. Seduction is a way of enticing or attracting approval and affection from another. Often sexual expression is the intercourse through which this acceptance is received and sexual attraction is mistaken as confirmation that they are loved.

Intimate TWOS make themselves attractive to others by adapting to their interests and agendas and supporting their bliss. TWOS are proud to be in the other's corner, which soon becomes their corner.

Love is thought of as melting resistance. There can be teasing and flirting associated with this style and often a desire for physical contact. Intimate TWOS frequently reach out and lightly touch people on the arm or hand to make a point or to connect with them.

Unfortunately, once the resistance is melted, things get boring. Because the real self is not touched, the personality has to go out and seduce others in an attempt to feel desirable and wanted.

*Aggression* represents a more direct attempt to overcome obstacles to the relationship and a more overt pushing for contact. Intimate TWOS may pick people who are unavailable to make the game more challenging and to mask their own paradoxical fear of intimacy. They are afraid that if others suspect the TWOS' have intimacy needs and aren't integrated, then others won't want to be with them.

Again, once the connection or conquest is made, the game is over and another pursuit must begin. The transaction is at the level of a social game between *personalities* and doesn't provide the real *self* with nourishment and satisfaction derived from genuine intimate contact between an I and a Thou.

If power is the ultimate aphrodisiac, then the Intimate TWOS' paradigm enables them to sense which people possess power. They then seek to seduce and connect with these influential individuals. Their pride wants them to be close to the power on the throne.

Similar to the intimate subtypes of other styles, the energy of the TWO is most evident in this subtype. They move into your space to help you, advise you, and intimately relate to you whether you need it or not. (Of course, you do need it; you just don't realize you do!)

Intimate TWOS can look like Intimate FOURS who are proud that their attractiveness will win others over to meet their needs.

## Style Three: The Effective Person

### Self Preservation Subtype

When deceit and personality get involved in the area of self preservation, **security** is sought through money, material possessions, status, and success. THREES erroneously believe they will survive because of the objects they possess. And if they possess the best brand names, they will survive more successfully. Even if you're not doing well, at least look like you are.

If money can't buy you love, maybe it can buy you identity, status, and security. For THREES, worth and approval come from work and earnings. When they are out of work, they've literally lost everything—including their self. So Self-preservation THREES work hard to assure job security.

Besides looking like they are hard-working, Self preservation THREES also want to represent the virtuous model of how a person should be. They want to be seen as good. Paradoxically they want to appear as though they are not concerned about appearance. This makes them the *countertype*. They are vain about not being vain. They can be confused with a Self preservation ONE or a SIX in that they are more anxious inside than other THREES.

Insecurity, though, never knows just how much is enough. Since lasting security is found only in one's essence or real self and in genuine I-Thou relationships, the personality stays on shaky ground, remains insecure because it is unreal, and must continue keeping its *mojo* working, performing well, increasing earnings, acquiring and consuming goods, belonging to successful organizations, etc.

### Social Subtype

When deceit contaminates the social instinct, the pursuit of **prestige** substitutes for or replaces a deeper desire for genuine interpersonal belonging. Personality masks the real self, fabricating an image that other personas can relate to. So, personality competes with personality rather than two genuine selves meeting in an I-Thou relationship. The result is show instead of engagement. What matters is to perform well in social roles to get social approval. Social status and rank, with their honors and endorsements, substitute for a missing sense of inner worth.

Social THREES are prone to vanity. They are concerned about what others think of them and are looking for a positive audience response such as: "You're doing fantastically." It's important to have the right credentials, to be a member of the right club, to be mentioned in social columns, to network with promising people. THREES are experts at adopting the appearance the group wants. *You're only as good as you look.*

While anonymity might be cherished by the FIVES' paradigm, it's tantamount to death in the THREES' world. And in contrast to the TWOS' song "You're nobody till somebody loves you," the THREES' lyrics are "You're nobody till somebody recognizes you." *I am seen, therefore I am.*

Because they are adept at spotting new developments, Social THREES become trend-setters by stepping to the forefront of popular movements and leading the bandwagon.

Social THREES can sometimes be confused with gregarious SEVENS.

**Intimate Subtype**

When the passion of deceit leaks into the sexual instinct, the result is a preoccupation about making a sexually appealing impression rather than being a genuinely sexual, loving person. The male wants to portray himself in the guise of the prevailing cultural expectation of what is **masculine**; while the female wants to appear as the current cultural **feminine** stereotype. Styles change. In the last 50 years in the United States, for example, women had to go from being buxom *ala* Marilyn Monroe to anorexic *ala* Twiggy to athletic *ala* Jane Fonda. In the meantime, men had to be romantic and verbal like Cary Grant, strong and seldom speaking like Clint Eastwood, then brawny and completely inarticulate like Sylvester Stallone.

The desire to appear as society expects one to be is prominent here. *Acting* sexual and *appearing* virile or feminine may replace *being* sexual and being genuinely in touch with one's masculinity and femininity. Playing the role of the sexual gigolo or gigolette is an attempt to get affirmation and approval for oneself. Playboy models represent the image of the perfect male and female.

Threes can be as competitive sexually as they are competitive in other areas of their lives. Whether they enjoy their sexuality or find any deeper meaning in it becomes secondary to a desire to appear sexually appealing.

This expression of an Intimate THREE might look like the Intimate TWO who overdoes being attractive. They can also look like an enthusiastic cheerleading SEVEN.

Employing a different cultural approach, the intimate THREE may appear as the "perfect wife or homemaker" or the "model husband and provider." If a more conservative society expects you to be a gentleman or a lady, then THREES will play that role. A Christian culture requires a different demeanor than does a Hollywood or Bollywood culture, for example. So, what image you assume and role you play depends on what segment of society you inhabit.

In the business world, Intimate THREES strive to be the top dog, top producer, top contender, top whatever. Appearing competent and confident are the keys to success.

# Style Four: The Original Person

## Self preservation subtype

When the passion of envy leaks into the instinct for self preservation, **dauntless**, reckless, risky behavior results.

Self preservation FOURS attempt to master their fears and depression through the repetition compulsion of recreating, by their own reckless actions, the possibility of loss. Acting impulsively without minding the consequences, they create energy for themselves by flirting on the edge of disaster like a drunk on a tightrope, living dangerously to get a sense of liveliness or to attract attention. More nervous than other FOURS, they are likely to jump off the edge of a cliff at the sound of a loud noise.

They want something or someone, acquire it, throw it away, then yearn for it again in a frustrating cycle of desire, loss, gain, loss, desire, etc.

Self preservation FOURS are determined to succeed in spite of their deficiencies. They have a sense of being flawed, but they are going to make it anyway. Even though their underlying sense is they are just not good enough, nonetheless they are determined to prevail. They will drive their way to success, defending themselves against their opponents or competition. They will not allow themselves to be intimidated, disheartened, or discouraged. With a need to endure, **tenacity** is another label for this subtype.

Often, they express a dutiful attitude, obedience to certain standards, or care for their family heritage. Their dauntless attitude gets expressed as: "Don't get in my way; I will do this if I want to; I have a responsibility to perform; I must defend and protect my family's tradition."

This is the *countertype*. They may not appear quite as envious as other FOURS or they may use comparisons to work harder to get what others have. They also keep their suffering to themselves more than other FOURS. They tough it out and are long-suffering vs. openly-suffering. They might also appear like SEVENS since they are lighter and sunnier and less melancholic than other FOURS.

## Social subtype

When the passion of envy enters and contaminates the social instinct, **shame** is the result. FOURS feel embarrassed that they have not measured up to their own elite standards or to their group's norms. Comparing themselves to others' achievements, FOURS feel woefully inadequate. They feel ashamed because they are not playing the social game well enough or because they have an inferior position or role in the game. Feeling bad about themselves and deeming themselves unworthy of love, they are hyper-sensitive to social slights. Believing they don't fit in or measure up, they sense there is no home or place for them.

Social FOURS are often convinced that others can intuit their inner deficiencies. For example, while walking down the street, FOURS may feel intense shame because they suspect that even strangers can see right through to their faults and flaws.

FOURS are particularly sensitive to feeling misunderstood and believe it is their destiny to suffer. However, they may do so in the shadows, because they don't want others to see their flaws.

This subtype is often confused or disoriented. Because they judge they don't measure up, they can feel humiliated and paralyzed in social groups and are afraid to speak lest they appear foolish. They share this fear with their next-door neighbors, the FIVES. Or, to compensate for their sense of inner turmoil, FOURS may rely more on their social image, their memberships in elite organizations, and other forms of public recognition—a feature they share with their other neighbors, the THREES.

Whereas the Intimate FOUR is mad, the Social subtype is sad. The Intimate FOUR can be complaining and demanding, the Social FOUR is more likely to suffer in silence. While the Social subtype is the most shameful, the Intimate FOUR is more shameless.

**Intimate subtype**

When the vice of envy leaks into and distorts sexuality, the resulting passion or driving force is **competition**. This competitiveness appears in all relationships but especially in intimate one-on-one pairings such as with one's mate where jealousy can also enter in. Intimate FOURS want to be the only person their partner has ever *really* loved. Or they want to be *the* special client of their therapist. FOURS may be competing *for* their loved one or competing *with* their loved one. They characteristically compare themselves with others, sizing up the competition, and then out-classing their competitor or mate. "I'll show you how good I am." Wanting to be considered worthy in the eyes of a significant other, FOURS operate from the assumption that: "If I best you, then you will respect me and find me desirable."

Sexual energy can be used in an attempt to win something from someone else, e.g. respect, appreciation, and approval. Sex can also be used to gain confidence as a compensation for feeling flawed, insufficient and ugly inside. Intimate FOURS can make themselves beautiful, charming, and elegant in the service of seducing someone and then turning them down. This is their attempt to manage their fears of abandonment: "I'll reject you before you can reject me."

To manage their depression and envy, FOURS may intensify their anger into hatred toward a competitor or spurning mate. Decreasing another's worth makes them less enviable and the FOUR more desirable.

This "feisty FOUR" may appear like an Intimate subtype EIGHT.

When Intimate FOURS turn their anger inward, they may have suicidal fantasies: "When I'm gone, you will realize what a wonderful person I was and you will realize what you have done to me."

Intimate FOURS are generally distinctive dressers whom you would expect to find on the pages of glamorous fashion magazines.

# Style Five: The Wise Person

## Self Preservation Subtype

When avarice leaks into the self preservation instinct, the result is the passionate seeking for a safe **refuge**, hiding place or home. Self preservation FIVES are looking for a **castle** to protect them from the invading world that easily seeps through their boundaries. Kafka's book *The Castle* captures this mode. They seek their own space where they can be alone, away from expectations and demands, where their ego feels secure. In this safe place, FIVES feel free to be themselves, to think, feel, and do what they want. It is very important for Self preservation FIVES to have their own space. In this secure hiding place, introverted FIVES can recharge their batteries and get re-energized to go back out into the world. It has been said that FIVES are looking for a "womb with a view," a warm cozy place where their needs are met and they can observe the world in unobstructed and unintruded bliss.

Self preservation FIVES may be the most boundaried of all the subtypes. As Robert Frost wrote: "Good fences make good neighbors."

Some Self preservation FIVES can be rather parsimonious, not asking for much and not taking much from the world. Since they don't ask for or fight for what they want, they make do with less.

**Social Subtype**

When the vice of avarice seeps into the social instinct, an attachment to **totems** appears. In place of relating freely and spontaneously from their essence, social FIVES interact with others through their false personality which relies on social archetypes, customs, roles, and rules for how to do things.

When something becomes a totem, the person or object is granted special respect. With Social FIVES, information or knowledge is given ascendance. In place of a totem pole standing outside their office, FIVES have their totems framed behind their desk, with their many sheepskins, degrees, and credentials hanging on the wall. FIVES may be deferred to for developing a special area of expertise. They seek power and recognition through understanding and mastering esoteric systems. This area of specialization provides them a niche in society where otherwise they might feel socially inferior or believe they have nothing to contribute. Having access to this secret knowledge gives Social FIVES a sense of power.

Their search for esoteric wisdom and the essence of life is an expression of their search for meaning which they share with other FIVES and also their FOUR neighbors.

Totems are objects that are given power beyond what they naturally possess. They can become objects of worship or addiction. For example collectors become attached to their collections of stamps, books, records, etc. FIVES' avarice gets codified in their collections. In the novel *The Collector*, a FIVE-like butterfly collector imprisons his totem love object, a young woman.

Social FIVES also like to align themselves with the source people of the tribe. They enjoy giving and getting advice from the inner circle and like to have inside information. Sharing this secret information, intellectual gossiping, is their way of being intimate.

FIVES want to be not just students but also confidants of their gurus. They want to be close to, or behind, positions of power: the King's confessor; the President's analyst; Arthur's Merlin, etc.

## Intimate Subtype

When the passion of avarice leaks into the sexual instinct, the resultant preoccupation is the drive to feel **confidence**. Sexual FIVES use sex in the service of augmenting confidence more than expressing love. With every sexual act, some assurance accrues. Surprisingly FIVES can express themselves passionately through sexuality where they may be reluctant to do so through verbal and emotional enunciations.

Intimate FIVES come out of themselves and are particularly confident and competent when playing prescribed roles. FIVE actors and actresses are often exemplars of this intimate subtype. When they are without a role, FIVES feel inadequate and vulnerable and so become diffident.

There can also be a bonding, an immediate intimacy, which happens through the exchange of confidences. No one else knows these secrets we have shared. This situation may be found in the intimacy of the confessional, the privacy of the therapist's office, or in the exchanges between confidants and lovers.

Intimate FIVES wear a look of confidence. They appear particularly cool and can be con-men and women, wolves in sheep's clothing, who seductively charm people to get what they want.

There is a forcefulness about FIVES' intellectual convictions: "If you think about this, you'll know I'm right." They can be intellectually arrogant and contemptuous of others. As Camus, an alleged FIVE, remarked: "There is no problem that cannot be overcome by contempt."

This is the *countertype*. Intimate FIVES want to be transparent with their ideal partner. Other subtypes are not quite as keen about being so visible. There is a romantic spirit in the depths of the Intimate FIVE and they might be avaricious about sharing their beloved with anyone else.

## Style Six: The Loyal Person

### Self Preservation Subtype

When the passion of fear interacts with the self preservation instinct, there is the attempt to ward off danger and fear by exhibiting **warmth** and friendliness. If you can get people to like you and see that you are no threat to them, then they won't want to hurt you and you don't have to be afraid of them. You can diffuse others' anger by winning their affection. Self preservation SIXES often have a cuddly little boy or girl quality about them. They can be warm and caring or ingratiating and flattering like TWOS and are often confused with the helpful Self preservation TWOS.

If you appear harmless, people won't feel threatened by you. So Self preservation SIXES are often self-deprecating and appear timid and fretful. They present a dependent or helpless mien.

Phobic and Self preservation SIXES are likely to show weakness to win others over, get others to protect them, and to discover whether they'll still like them after they've exposed their vulnerable side. On the other hand, Counter-Fearful and Intimate SIXES are more likely to relate with a show of strength, challenging and provoking others to ascertain if they're trustworthy. Both interpersonal gambits represent attempts to lessen the SIXES' anxieties and fears.

Self preservation SIXES are often funny individuals with a self-effacing persona like Woody Allen's. Like other Self preservation subtypes, this sub group is more anxious and self-contained than the more extraverted Social or Intimate subtypes.

Like their neighbors, the Self-preservation FIVES, SIXES may view their home as a safe haven against the assaults of the outside world. Barricaded inside they feel protected and warmed. The problem with castles, you either get bored or starved to death if you stay inside too long.

**Social Subtype**
When the passion of fear leaks into the social instinct, you secure your place in the group by doing your **duty** and by following the rules of the game. Spontaneous I-Thou mutual interactions are replaced by officially

sanctioned behaviors. If you do what is required, you will be accepted into the group and not expelled from it. Social SIXES do what others expect of them. They tend to be obedient, conservative, and of an authoritarian mind. They are searching to do the father's, commander's, or superior's will. Like Hamlet, they have a duty to perform to honor their father. Social SIXES believe that group cohesiveness will be established and maintained by adhering to rules and protocol, engaging in socially acceptable behavior, and manifesting uniformity. Social SIXES tend to be "company men and women."

Social SIXES are gracious and diplomatic. They want others to feel comfortable. They expect the best from people and give others their best.

On the other hand, those who don't follow policy and procedure might be hounded and drummed out of the organization. And those with alternative worldviews might be persecuted or rehabilitated according to the group's values and visions.

With their eye for detail, concern for efficiency, and their legalistic approach, Social SIXES can look like THREES, or more likely, ONES.

### Intimate Subtype

When the passion of fear leaks into the sexual instinct, the result is an attempt to contain or compensate for that fear through acquiring **strength** and acting threatening for males and by possessing **beauty** and becoming sexually alluring and seductive for females. You might recognize these as some of the tricks of the THREE trade, whose paradigm SIXES may utilize under stressful conditions. By looking strong or attractive, SIXES lessen their anxiety about feeling weak or ugly. Intimate SIXES may seek to ally with strong or beautiful partners for protection. When SIXES feel secure with their partner, they are not as fearful.

Intimate SIXES are likely to become soldiers or practice the martial arts. Often, but not always, Counter-Phobic SIXES are sexual subtypes who use antagonism and intimidation as a pre-emptive tactic. Their image can hold others at bay. Men pursue some counter-phobic feat of strength; women play the part of the *femme fatal.*

Counter-phobic SIXES impulsively do the very thing they are afraid of vs. avoid those things if they are a Phobic SIX. If the former is afraid of heights, they will take up sky-diving; while the latter will take a train.

Not surprisingly, this is the *countertype.* They are attracted to intrigue and danger and may become involved in counter-cultural groups and movements. In this way they look like EIGHTS.

## Style Seven: The Joyful Person

### Self preservation subtype

When gluttony meets self-preservation, you have the attempt to maintain security by belonging to a group of **like-minded people** who believe in, pursue, and defend the same things you do. The television series *Cheers* portrays this kind of Self-preservation SEVEN atmosphere where the extended family of friends at the bar becomes as important as, or more important than, one's family of origin or nuclear family. The internal sanctuary sought by the FIVE and SIX Self-preservation subtypes becomes exteriorized into the safe refuge of the extended family for the Self-preservation SEVEN. This subtype has also been labeled **keepers of the castle**.

Liking to travel the party circuit, Self-preservation SEVENS are attracted to communes, social committees, drinking buddies, tour clubs or other groups that convene and have fun together. They evince a "hale fellow well met" disposition, looking for a slap on the back and no serious questions. They are looking for a safe place where interesting things happen.

### Social subtype

Oddly enough, when the passion of gluttony leaks into the social arena, SEVENS will **sacrifice** their options and limit their possibilities for the sake of their family or whatever community they belong to. This is the SEVENS' version of the Social SIXES' sense of *duty*. Their obligations to others' welfare place limits on their personal possibilities. This also curtails their gluttony, but only temporarily. For SEVENS hope that once everyone is happy or once their children are grown, they can get on with actualizing all their possibilities.

It's nice to be with interesting and stimulating people who share the same vision and goals. Unfortunately sometimes group endeavors can be tedious **martyr-**

making events. Social SEVENS accept these **social limitations** in order to work with congenial groups. They are willing to give up or sacrifice certain personal freedoms to pursue their ideals within their family, political group, or religion—somewhat reminiscent of the ONES' idealism.

The social theory of Jean Jacques Rousseau, the eighteenth-century political philosopher, informs this subtype variation. Recall Rousseau's belief and lament that society's restrictions are the cause of human suffering and depravity. Once we remove society's limits on our free self-expression and development, we revert to being the happy, benevolent, "noble savages" we really are. Humanistic psychology shares this optimistic air.

This is the *countertype*, since sacrifice is not the first word that comes to mind for other SEVENS. Social SEVENS can be confused with TWOS, in that both like to be of service (at least for a time.)

### Intimate subtype

When the passion of gluttony contaminates the sexual instinct, the result is the state of **suggestibility** and **fascination**—especially with new relational possibilities. Ideas arise and are accepted or acted upon readily and uncritically. And SEVENS usually have more ideas than they know what to do with. What comes to mind as a suggestion or possibility quickly gains credibility as a reality. Intimate SEVENS can be easily talked into anything and may get into something over their heads before soberly considering what they're doing. Their initial fascination makes them enthusiastic promoters of processes, products, and places they little understand.

The state of "monkey mind" is particularly prevalent in this intimate subtype. The mind jumps impulsively from one interesting thought to another, distracted and knocked off course by anything new.

They are optimistic dreamers who live in the world of imagination.

While all SEVENS like variety, Intimate SEVENS especially crave it. They are fascinated with the new and exotic. Both their attention span and their relationships tend to be brief. They have intense but short-lived experiences.

Intimate SEVENS like to roam to see new places and have new adventures. They tend to be world travelers who check in with you on their loops around the planet, becoming bored if they settle down for too long.

Intimate SEVENS can be prone to Don Juanism, sexual promiscuity, and experimentation. Sexual "trips" are more interesting and exciting than long-term relationships. Experiments with homosexuality, bisexuality, and other variations are not uncommon among Intimate SEVENS.

In the manner of the FOURS' style, Intimate SEVENS can romanticize their relationships to avoid the tedium and limitations of their daily interactions. They project their fantasies onto their partners and act them out instead of engaging the real person.

# Style Eight: The Powerful Person

## Self-Preservation Subtype

When the passion of lust leaks into the self-preservation instinct, the resultant disposition is that of **satisfactory survival**. Things are tough, the going is difficult, but you're making it. It's not terrific, but you have enough of everything you want. Coping substitutes for self preservation; covering your survival needs replaces attending to your higher needs. Self-preservation EIGHTS live at the bottom of Maslow's need hierarchy, taking care of survival and safety needs while neglecting to climb the ladder to relational, self actualizing, and self transcending needs. As long as your basic needs are met, and your supply lines are established, you're doing O.K. You don't need anybody else; you can make it on your own. If you have control over your immediate surroundings, if you have a "clean, well lighted place" as Hemingway wrote, you'll be all right.

Self-preservation EIGHTS are often found in survivalist movements. They are fixated on personally guaranteeing their self preservation instead of trusting in the goodness of the universe—or at least of their neighbor. Wanting to control their piece of the planet, they fortify their castle against nuclear attack. In this Darwinian environment, only the strong survive.

The **satisfaction** label refers to the EIGHTS wanting their material needs met right away. Frustration is not something they countenance for long. They are good at bargaining for what they want. And may even make you an offer you can't refuse.

They might look like Intimate ONES, though ONES are over-concerned about norms while EIGHTS are under-concerned.

### Social Subtype

When the passion of lust combines with the social instinct, the result is a strong attraction and devotion to **friendships**. In this dog eat dog world, you need to have friends you can rely on. Social EIGHTS are friends for life. They will take care of you and be there when you need them. They take great satisfaction from their relationships with their pals and cronies. Street gangs, social clubs, and cliques are frequent habitats of Social EIGHTS. **Solidarity** is a value for this subtype.

You know where you stand with tested comrades and you can let your feelings out with them, often late into the night. Being loyal to friends is a hallmark of the Social EIGHT. There is an addictive overdone quality to their passionate friendships where power and control subtly substitute for mutual intimacy and vulnerability: "I'll protect you and you protect me and we'll make it in this world."

In Hemingway's novels, which are usually peopled by EIGHTS, friendship is often the topic of conversation or the essence of the plot.

Individuals who are in need of protection or strength are often attracted to Social EIGHTS. This is the *countertype* who is concerned with social justice, community organizing, standing up for the underdog and the vulnerable. This softer EIGHT can be confused with the Social TWO.

### Intimate Subtype
When the passion of lust leaks into the sexual instinct, the result is the attempt to possess the earth, or at least one's own turf, mate, children, employees, etc. **Possession** means intense involvement in and taking charge of others' lives and is the EIGHTS' substitute for genuine closeness.

Contests for control are ways of connecting with others. If others stand their ground, and remain forthright, strong, and respectful (i.e., if they respond like EIGHTS), then maybe they can be trusted and EIGHTS can surrender some control.

When Eights move to the downside of the TWO, they obsess over their partner and, if they become suspicious besides, may become stalking and vengeful. Their aggressive pursuit disguises an underlying dependency.

Intimate EIGHTS tend to be the delinquent kids (or adults) on the block (or in the firm). They are the rebels with or without a cause. They tend to squeeze the life out of things and use them up: "You only go through life once, so live it with all the gusto you can." They like fast cars, vast amounts of liquor, and anything else they can consume. Control and possession become ways to avoid anxiety, vulnerability, and intimacy.

The issue of who's on top, who's in charge, who's ultimately in control, is a lively one for Intimate EIGHTS who find surrender an extremely difficult gesture.

This is a very intense passionate EIGHT who can sometimes look like an intense passionate Intimate FOUR.

## Style Nine: The Peaceful Person

### Self-Preservation Subtype

When the vice of indolence leaks into the self-preservation instinct, **appetite** gets divorced from satisfaction, can grow out of control, and be pursued for its own sake. Binge-eating or drinking, shopping sprees, trips to the casino, etc. are conflict-resolving strategies for NINES, allowing them to numb out while appearing to be active.

Self-preservation NINES surround themselves with things but then don't use them. They collect comfort items and set things up the way they like them, then never quite get around to them. Or they can over-identify or lose themselves in their routines and collectibles. This expression of indolence helps them avoid the real issues, priorities, and conflicts they need to address. They distract themselves with inconsequentials and don't attend to their personal business.

They lower their expectations of life and settle for physical ease, comforting routines, and limited horizons. Asking little from life, Self-preservation NINES appreciate what they have and don't rock the boat or upset the apple cart. Simple pleasures provide reassurance and substitute for love. Zoning out on food or blanking out in front of the TV help time pass effortlessly. The term "couch potato" was quite possibly coined for this subtype.

Minor activities can drain the energy of self-preservation NINES: "I cleaned out my desk drawer this morning and had to take the rest of the day off."

Self-preservation NINES numb their injured egos through appetite and distraction rather than satisfying their real self through attending to essential business. They deal with anger and anxiety through appetite, trying to either drown these feelings or stuff them. The ego wishes for inconsequential things it thinks it needs for survival, replacing true needs and desires with non-essentials. But these wishes don't fulfill the real self, which still experiences a hunger that never was and still isn't fulfilled.

**Social Subtype**

When the vice of indolence distorts the social instinct, the result is **social participation**. Groups give NINES a sense of inclusion and belonging. They get attention and feel loved and energized in groups. At the same time they are ambivalent about groups. Social NINES join and lose themselves in groups but also resist group influence and expectations by not getting completely involved or becoming fully committed. Hanging around the fringes, they participate in groups only half-heartedly, never being really fully present, yet never dropping out, either.

Social NINES often find themselves in groups as a way of avoiding their own agendas or distracting themselves from doing what they really need to do. Social NINES can get into trial marriages which last for 20 years. As inertia sets in, they never quite find the energy to leave. Or it's not that they don't love their spouse, they just can't find the energy to express it.

Social NINES get excitement through the energy of people doing things together. They can tap into this energy to enliven themselves and can easily become "groupies."

As with all nine types, the ego or false personality tries to interact with other egos in social games while the true self or essence seeks to participate in genuine interpersonal relationships.

Since Social NINES can get busy in groups to avoid working on themselves and can lose themselves in their service to others, this is the *countertype* who can be confused with hard-working THREES or self-emptying TWOS.

**Intimate Subtype**

When the vice of indolence leaks into and influences the sexual instinct, the result is the desire for **union** or **fusion** with another. This is a distortion of true sexual union, which is an expression of a genuine *I-Thou* relationship where there is a self-in-relationship. NINES seek to merge with an undemanding other in whom they can lose themselves and who will take care of them in an effortless belonging. Rather than highlighting their uniqueness and individuality, NINES blur their boundaries and meld into the beloved, in something like an *it-it* relationship where neither partner feels very unique or special. In Gestalt therapy terms, this is the defense mechanism of confluence. Instead of merging with others, NINES need to first differentiate themselves and then make genuine contact with differentiated others.

Intimate NINES are attempting to regain their lost sense of identity, belonging, and sense of connection to the cosmos by becoming one with the other and living in and through the other. Feeling incomplete and cut off from life, they hope another's love will help them be noticed, be somebody, be whole, and be united. NINES become someone else instead of coming close to someone else. The other person's agenda can replace their own. A merged sense of *we* replaces *I-Thou*. Dan Siegel talks about MWE which is a healthy combination of ME and THEE to make a MWE. NINES need to let their ME grow before they integrate into a WE.

# Bibliography

## Books about the Enneagram

### General Introduction

Baron, Renee, Elizabeth Wagele. *The Enneagram Made Easy*. San Francisco: Harper San Francisco, 1994.

———. *Are You My Type? Am I Yours?* San Francisco: Harper San Francisco, 1994.

Beesing, Maria, Robert Nogosek, Patrick O'Leary. *The Enneagram: a Journey of Self Discovery*. Denville, N.J.: Dimension Bks, 1984.

Brady, Loretta. *Beginning Your Enneagram Journey*. Thomas More, 1994.

———. *Finding Yourself on the Enneagram*. Thomas More, 1997.

Carlini, John. *Maximizing Your Enneagram Type: a Workbook*. Highwood, IL: Center of Growth Publications, 2014.

Chestnut, Beatrice. *The Complete Enneagram: 27 Paths to Greater Self-Knowledge*. Berkeley CA: She Writes Press, 2013.

Christlieb, Fatima Fernandez. *Where on Earth Did the Enneagram Come From?* Lightning Source, 2016.

Hurley, Kathleen, and Theodore Dobson. *What's My Type?* San Francisco: Harper Collins, 1991.

———. *My Best Self: Using the Enneagram to Free the Soul.* San Francisco: Harper/San Francisco, 1993.

———. *Discover Your Soul Potential: Using the Enneagram to Awaken Spiritual Vitality.* Lakewood, CO: WindWalker Press, 2000.

Landis, Ruthie. *Beyond the Bookclub: We Are the Books We Must Read*: Columbus, OH: Gatekeeper Press, 2018

Naranjo, Claudio. *The Enneagram of Society*: Nevada City, CA: Gateways, 2004.

Palmer, Helen. *The Enneagram.* San Francisco: Harper and Row, 1988.

Pearce, Herb, with Karen Brees. *The Complete Idiot's Guide to the Power of the Enneagram.* New York: Alpha Books, 2007.

Reynolds, Susan. *The Everything Enneagram Book.* Avon, MA: F+W Media, 2007.

Rhodes, Susan. *The Positive Enneagram.* Seattle: Geranium Press, 2009.

———. *Archetypes of the Enneagram.* Seattle: Geranium Press, 2010.

———. *The Integral Enneagram.* Seattle: Geranium Press, 2013.

Riso, Don Richard. *Personality Types: Using the Enneagram for Self Discovery.* Boston: Houghton Mifflin, 1996.

———. *Understanding the Enneagram.* Boston: Houghlin Mifflin, 1990.

Thomson, Clarence and Thomas Condon (Eds). *Ennea-gram Applications: Personality Styles in Business, Therapy, Medicine, and Daily Life*. Portland, OR: Metamorphous Press, 2001.

Wagner, Jerome. *The Enneagram Spectrum of Personality Styles*. Evanston IL: NineLens Press, 1996.

————. *Nine Lenses on the World: The Enneagram Perspective*. Evanston IL: NineLens Press, 2010.

Webb, Karen. *The Enneagram*. London: Thorsons, 1996.

Zanos, Susan. *Human Types: Essence and the Enneagram*. Boston: Weiser Books, 1997.

## The Enneagram in the Arts, Film, and Literature

Condon, Thomas. *The Enneagram Movie and Video Guide, 2nd Ed. Rev.* Portland: Metamorphous Press, 1999.

Goldberg, Michael. *Travels with Odysseus: Uncommon Wisdom from Homer's Odyssey*. Tempe: Circe's Island Press, 2005

Searle, Judith. *The Literary Enneagram*. Portland: Metamorphous Press, 2001.

Schnebly, Lauri. *Believable Characters: Creating with Enneagrams*. Tucson AZ: Cider Press, 2007.

## The Enneagram and Business

Apple, Wendy. *InsideOut Enneagram: the Game-Changing Guide for Leaders*. San Rafael, CA: Palma Publishing, 2011.

Bast, Mary, and Clarence Thomson. *Out of the Box: Coaching with the Enneagram*. Portland: Stellar Attractions, 2003.

Cloete, Dirk. *Integrative Enneagram for Practitioners*: South Africa: ABC Press, 2019

David, Oscar. *The Enneagram for Managers*. Lincoln, NE: Writers Club Press, 2001.

Goldberg, Michael. *Getting Your Boss's Number*. San Francisco: HarperSan Francisco, 1996.

Howe-Murphy, Roxanne. *Deep Coaching: Using the Enneagram as a Catalyst for Profound Change*. El Grenada CA: Enneagram Press, 2007.

———. *Deep Living: Transforming Your Relationship to Everything that Matters through the Enneagram*. Santa Fe, NM: Enneagram Press, 2013.

Lapid-Bogda, Ginger. *Bringing Out the Best in Yourself at Work*. New York: McGraw-Hill, 2004.

———. *What Type of Leader Are You?* New York: McGraw-Hill, 2007.

———. *Bringing Out the Best in Everyone You Coach*. New York: McGraw-Hill, 2009.

Lazenby, Malcolm and Gayle Hardie. *Working with Emotional Health and the Enneagram*: Australia: Monterey Press, 2019

Nathans, Hannah. *The Enneagram at Work*. The Netherlands: Scriptum Schiedam, 2003.

Palmer Helen. *The Enneagram in Love and Work:* New York: HarperCollins, 1995.

———. *The Enneagram Advantage*: New York: Harmony Books, 1998.

Tallon, Robert, and Mario Sikora. *From Awareness to Action*. Scranton: University of Scranton Press, 2004.

## The Enneagram and Careers

Wagele, Elizabeth and Stabb, Ingrid. *The Career Within You*. New York: Harper One, 2010.

## The Enneagram and Children

Wagele Elizabeth. *Finding the Birthday Cake: Helping Children Raise Their Self-Esteem*. Far Hills, N.J.: New Horizon Press, 2007

## The Enneagram and Death

Wagele, Elizabeth. *The Enneagram of Death: Helpful Insights by the 9 Types of People on Grief, Fear, and Dying*. International Enneagram Association, 2012.

## The Enneagram and Learning

Callahan, William. *The Enneagram for Youth: Student Edition and Counselor's Manual*. Chicago, Loyola University Press, 1992.

Levine, Janet. *The Enneagram Intelligences*. New York: Greenwood Publishing Group, 1998.

## The Enneagram and Parenting

Levine, Janet. *Know Your Parenting Personality*. Hoboken: Wiley & Sons 2003.

Tressider, Tacy; Loftus, Margaret; Pollock, Jacqui. *Knowing Me, Knowing Them: Understand Your Parenting Personality by Discovering the Enneagram*. Carlton North VIC, Australia, 2014

Wagele Elizabeth. *The Enneagram of Parenting*. San Francisco: HarperSanFrancisco, 1998.

## The Enneagram and Relationships

Baron, Renee and Wagele, Elizabeth. *Are You My Type, Am I Yours?: Relationships Made Easy Through the Enneagram*. San Francisco: HarperOne, 1995.

Coates, Mona and Searle, Judith. *Sex, Love, and Your Personality: The Nine Faces of Intimacy*. Santa Monica CA: Therapy Options Press, 2011.

Coates, Mona. *Keeping Love Alive: Tools that Work for Couples*. Santa Monica, CA: Therapy Options Press, 2018.

Daniels, David and Suzanne Dion. *The Enneagram, Relationships and Intimacy*: 2019.

Schneider, Jennifer, and Corn, Ron. *Understand Yourself, Understand Your Partner: The Essential Enneagram Guide to a Better Relationship*. CreateSpace Independent Publishing Plaform, 2013.


## The Enneagram and Spirituality

Addison, Howard. *The Enneagram and Kabbalah*. Woodstock, VT: Jewish Lights Publishing, 1998.

Almaas, A.H. *Facets of Unity: the Enneagram of Holy Ideas.*. Berkeley: Diamond Books, 1998.

Bergin, Eilis, and Eddie Fitzgerald. *An Enneagram Guide: A Spirituality of Love in Brokenness*. Mystic, CT: Twenty Third Publications, 1992.

Calhoun, Adele and Doug and Clare and Scott Loughrige. *Spiritual Rhythms for the Enneagram: a Handbook for Harmony and Transformation*. Downers Grove, IL: InterVarsity Press, 2019.

Cron, Ian and Suzanne Stabile. *The Road Back to You: an Enneagram Journey to Self-Discovery.* Downers Grove, IL: InterVarsity Press, 2016.

Empereur, James. *The Enneagram and Spiritual Direction: Nine Paths to Spiritual Guidance.*, New York: Crossroad, 1997.

Falikowski, Anthony. *Higher Reality Therapy: Nine Pathways to Inner Peace,* Winchester:UK, 2010

Fryling, Alice. *Mirror for the Soul: a Christian Guide to the Enneagram.* Downers Grove, IL: InterVarsity Press, 2017.

Gotch, Carol Ann and David Walsh. *Soul Stuff: Reflections on Inner Work with the Enneagram.* Vermett, Manitoba, CA: Inscapes Publications, 1994.

Henry, Kathleen. *The Book of Enneagram Prayers.* Boulder, CO: Woven Word Press, 1991.

Hey, David. *The 9 Dimensions of the Soul: Essence and the Enneagram.* Winchester, UK: O Books, 2006.

Howell, Joseph. *Becoming Conscious: the Enneagram's Forgotten Passageway* (2nd Ed.). Bloomington, IN: Balboa Press, 2014.

Huertz, Christopher. *The Sacred Enneagram: Finding Your Unique Path to Spiritual Growth.* Grand Rapids, MI: Zondervan, 2017.

———. *The Enneagram of Belonging: a Compassionate Journey of Self-Acceptance.* Grand Rapids, MI: Zondervan, 2020.

Jaxon-Bear, Eli. *The Enneagram of Liberation: from Fixation to Freedom,* Bolinas, CA: Leela Foundation Press, 2001.

Maitri, Sandra. *The Spiritual Dimension of the Ennea-gram*. New York: Tarcher/Putnam, 2000.

————. *The Enneagram of Passions and Virtues*. New York: Tarcher/Putnam, 2005.

Metz, Barbara, and John Burchill. *The Enneagram and Prayer*. Denville, N.J.: Dimension Bks, 1987.

Mortz, Mary. Overcoming Our Compulsions: Using the Twelve Steps and the Enneagram as Spiritual Tools for Life. Chicago: Triumph Books, 1994.

Nogosek, Robert. *Nine Portraits of Jesus*. Denville, N.J.: Dimension Bks, 1985.

————. The Enneagram Journey to New Life. Denville, N.J.: Dimension Bks, 1995.

Riso, Don Richard and Russ Hudson *The Wisdom of the Enneagram: The Psychology and Spirituality of Trans-formation*. New York: Bantam, 1999.

Rohr, Richard, and Andreas Ebert. *Discovering the Enneagram*. New York: Crossroad, 1990.

————. *Experiencing the Enneagram*. New York: Cross-road, 1992.

————. *The Enneagram: a Christian Perspective*. New York: Crossroad, 2002.

Schafer, William. *Roaming Free Inside the Cage: a Daoist Approach to the Enneagram and Spritirual Transforma-tion*. Luniverse, 2010.

Thomson, Clarence. *Parables and the Enneagram*. New York: Crossroad, 1996.

Tickerhoof, Bernard. *Conversion and the Enneagram*. Denville, N.J.: Dimension Bks, 1991.

Vancil, Marilyn. *Self to Lose, Self to Find: a Biblical Approach to the 9 Enneagram Types*. Emumclaw, WA.: Redemption Press, 2016.

Zuercher, Suzanne. *Enneagram Spirituality*. Notre Dame, IN: Ave Maria Press, 1992.

———. *Enneagram Companions*. Notre Dame, IN: Ave Maria Press, 1993.

———. *Merton: and Enneagram Profile*. Notre Dame, IN: Ave Maria Press, 1993.

## The Enneagram and Teens

Wagele Elizabeth. *The Enneagram of Teens: Discover Your Personality Type and Celebrate Your True Self*. PLI Media, 2014.

## The Enneagram and Therapy

Bartlett, Carolyn. *The Enneagram Field Guide*. Nine Gates Publishing, 2007.

Keyes, Margaret. *Emotions and the Enneagram*. Muir Beach, CA: Molysdatur Publ., 1992, Rev. Ed.

Landis, Ruthie. *Beyond the Bookclub: We Are the Books We Must Read*. Columbus, OH: Gatekeeper Press, 2018.

Lyleson, Eric. *Essential Wholeness: Integral Psychotherapy, Spiritual Awakening, and the Enneagram*. Bloomington, IN: Balboa Press,2015.

Naranjo, Claudio. *Ennea-type Structures*. Nevada City, CA: Gateways, 1990.

———. *Character and Neurosis: An Integrative View*. Nevada City, CA: Gateways, 1994.

———. *Enneatypes in Psychotherapy*. Nevada City, CA: Gateways, 1994.

———. *Transformation through Insight: Enneatypes in Life, Literature and Clinical Practice*. Prescott, AZ: Hohm Press, 1997.

Linden, Anne, Murray Spalding. *The Enneagram and NLP*. Portland: Metamorphous Press, 1994.

Wolinsky, Stephen. *The Tao of Chaos: Essence and the Enneagram*. Connecticut: Bramble Books, 1994.


**Enneagram Inventories**

Daniels, David, and Virginia Price. *The Essential Enneagram Revised*. San Francisco: HarperSanFrancisco, 2009.

Lapid-Bogda, Ginger. *The Art of Typing: Powerful Tools for Enneagram Typing*. Santa Monica, CA: Enneagram in Business Press, 2018

Riso, Don. *Discovering Your Personality Type*. New York: Houghton Mifflin, 1992.

Wagner, Jerome. *Wagner Enneagram Personality Style Scales*. Los Angeles: Western Psychological Services, 1999. www.wepss.com


**Enneagram Research**

The Enneagram Journal (Volumes 1–6). International Enneagram Association. www.internationalenneagram .org

Abdullah, M. (n.d.). *The RHETI Enneagram test*. (Unpublished master's thesis). University of Baghdad, Baghdad, Iraq.

Albert, J. L. (2011). *First-generation female higher education student affairs personnel: The significance of personality and spirituality*. (Unpublished doctoral dissertation). Capella University, Minneapolis, MN.

Andre, S. (2014). *Reliability and validation study of the Online Instinctual Variant Questionnaire*. (Unpublished doctoral dissertation). Florida Atlantic University, Boca Raton, FL.

Arthur, K. B. (2008). *Attachment styles and enneagram types: Development and testing of an integrated model for use in marriage and family therapy*. (Unpublished doctoral dissertation). Virginia Polytechnic Institute and State University, Blacksburg, VA.

Arthur, K. & Allen, K. (2010). The nature of love: Understanding the Enneagram types as nine expressions of attachment. *The Enneagram Journal*, 3(1), 6–22.

Bartman, D., & Brown, A. (2005). *Putting the person into personality: SHL Short research report 2005*. SHL White paper.

Beauvais, P. M. (1973). *Claudio Naranjo and SAT: A modern manifestation of Sufism?* (Unpublished doctoral dissertation). The Hartford Seminary Foundation, Litchfield, CT.

Becker, M. (1992). Empirical studies of the enneagram: Foundations and comparison. In A. Ebert & M. Kustemacher (Eds.), *Experiencing the enneagram* (P. Heinegg, Trans.). New York: Crossroad.

Bland, A. M. (2018). Facilitating and assessing personal growth in helper development using Hart's (2014) four virtues. *The Humanistic Psychologist*, 46, 6–29.

Brent, B. P. (1994). *A quantitative and descriptive study of distinct and self-consistent attentional styles and their relation to Enneagram typology.* (Unpublished doctoral dissertation). Institute of Transpersonal Psychology, Palo Alto, CA.

Brown, A., & Bartram, D. (2005). Relationships between OPQ and Enneagram types. Surrey, UK: SHL Group.

Brooks, D. (1998). Are personality traits inherited? *South African Journal of Science, 94,* 9–11. Carpenter, D. (2015). *Resonating personality types for couples: An Enneagram application for predicting marital satisfaction.* (Unpublished doctoral dissertation). Walden University, Minneapolis, MN.

Chawla, B. (1999). *A critical inquiry in to Enneagram as an ancient technique for judging personality types.* (Unpublished doctoral dissertation). Maharaja Sayajirao University of Baroda (India).

Chiang, C. (2011). *A study of the relationship between team members' personalities and cultural dimensions and their effects on team performance.* (Unpublished doctoral dissertation). Benedictine University, Lisle, IL.

Choucroun, P. M. (2012). *An exploratory analysis of the enneagram typology in couple counseling: A qualitative analysis.* (Unpublished doctoral dissertation). University of Texas at San Antonio, San Antonio, TX.

Clayton, T. L. (2014). *Clergy spiritual assessment using the Enneagram.* (Unpublished doctoral dissertation). Garrett-Evangelical Theological Seminary, Evanston, IL.

Cluley, W. H. (2005). *Vital gifts and veiled temptations: Using the enneagram to understand holy identity*. (Unpublished doctoral dissertation). Lancaster Theological Seminary, Lancaster, PA.

Coker, C. & Mihai, F. (2017). Personality traits and second language acquisition: The influence of the Enneagram on adult ESOL students. *TESOL Journal*, 8(2), 432–449.

Cowan, P. (2006). *The Enneagram: An action research project to establish the efficacy of introducing the Enneagram, a model of personality, as an intervention to a team*. (Unpublished master's thesis). University of Surrey, Surrey, UK.

Dameyer, J. J. (2001). *Psychometric evaluation of the Riso-Hudson Enneagram Type Indicator*. California Institute of Integral Studies, San Francisco, CA.

Daniels, D., & Price, V. (2000). *Essential enneagram: The definitive personality test and self-discovery guide (Revised & Updated)*. New York: Harper Collins.

Daniels, D., Saracino, T., Fraley, M., Christian, J., & Pardo, S. (2018). Advancing ego development in adulthood through study of the Enneagram system of personality. *Journal of Adult Development*, 25, 229–241.

Delobbe, N., Halin, P., Premont, J., & Wuidar, D. (n.d.). *Measuring personality at work: Development and validation of a new instrument (HPEI) based on the Enneagram*. Louvain School of Management, Belgium.

Dimond, A. M. (2013). *Because minds can't sit in classrooms without bodies: Making use of the Enneagram as a tool for embodied education*. (Unpublished master's thesis). Creighton University, Omaha, NE.

Doss, J. L. (1995). *Spiritual growth through small groups: A synthesis of group psychotherapy and spiritual direction to enhance Christian wholeness.* (Unpublished doctoral dissertation). Drew University, Madison, NJ.

Dye, M. J. (1997). *God's word for every heart: Exegesis through Enneagram types.* (Unpublished doctoral dissertation). Drew University, Madison, NJ.

Edwards, A. C. (1991). Clipping the wings off the enneagram: A study in people's perceptions of a ninefold personality typology. *Social Behavior and Personality, 19,* 11–20.

Enneagram in Business Network. (2011). Benchmark report. Retrieved from https://theenneagraminbusiness .com/wp-content/uploads/2013/10/ENGLISH-EnneagramBenchmarkReport2011.pdf

Flautt, T. (1998). MBTI-Enneagram type correlation study results. *Bulletin of Psychological Type, 21*(8), 37–38.

Flautt, T., & Richards, J. (1997a). Finding meaning in MBTI and Enneagram type correlations. *Bulletin of Psychological Type, 20*(4), 32–34.

Flautt, T., & Richards, J. (1997b). Preliminary report: MBTI-Enneagram study. *Bulletin of Psychological Type, 20*(2), 39.

Flautt, T. & Richards, J. (1998). *MBTI and Enneagram: Their relationship and complementary use.* Retrieved from http://www.goconscious.com/home/articles/tom-flautt.html on February 14, 2020.

Gallant, H. (2005). *The use of the Enneagram to improve customer relationships with a motor vehicle manufacturer.*

(Unpublished master's thesis). Nelson Mandela Metropolitan University, Port Elizabeth, South Africa.

Gamard, W. S. (1986). *Interrater reliability and validity of judgments of enneagram personality types.* (Unpublished doctoral dissertation). California Institute of Integral Studies, San Francisco, CA.

Giordano, M. E. (2008). *A psychometric evaluation of the Riso-Hudson Type Indicator (RHETI), version 2.5: Comparison of ipsative and non-ipsative versions and correlations with spiritual outcomes.* (Unpublished doctoral dissertation). Loyola College in Maryland, Baltimore, MD.

Godin, J. (2010). *The effect of the Enneagram on psychological well-being and unconditional self-acceptance of young adults.* Iowa State University, Ames, IA.

Havens, S. E. (1995). *Comparisons of Myers-Briggs and Enneagram types of registered nurses.* (Unpublished doctoral dissertation). University of Florida, Gainesville, FL.

Hebenstreit, R. K. (2007). *Using the Enneagram to help organizations attract, motivate, and retain their employees.* (Unpublished doctoral dissertation.) Alliant International University, San Francisco, CA.

Hebenstreit, R. K. (2008). A call to apply the principles of the Enneagram in organizations to attract, retain, and motivate employees. *The Enneagram Journal*, 1(1), 4–21.

Ho, G. (2018). *The box is where we began: Evaluating Enneagram-based leadership development for catholic school leaders in Indonesia.* (Unpublished doctoral dissertation). Lamar University, Beaumont, TX.

Huber, M. G. (1999). Myers-Briggs type indicator correlations with enneatype-6 alcohol or other drug
clients in clinical settings in Southeastern Wiscon-
sin. *Journal of Ministry in Addiction and Recovery*, 6,
75–97.

Johnson, J. D. (2019). *The connection between lead pastors'
Enneagram personality type and congregational size.*
(Unpublished doctoral dissertation). Southeastern
University, Lakeland, FL.

Kim, S. M., Ryu, C. S., & Chung, J. I. (2016). The
effects of enneagram personality types in the robot
programming classes centering around the robot
department students of a technical high school.
*International Journal of u- and e-Service, Science and
Technology*, 9(9), 121–128.

Kim, S. Y., Ahn, S. Y., & Koh, A. R. (2016). Fashion
consumers' purchase decision-making styles related
to Enneagram core values and self-construal levels.
*Family and Environmental Research*, 54(2), 207–225.

Kingma, M. (2007). *Utilising a personality typology to
resolve subliminal conflict in the workplace.* (Unpublished doctoral dissertation). Cape Peninsula University of Technology, Cape Town, South Africa.

Komasi, S., Soroush, A., Nazeie, N., Saeidi, M., &
Zakiei, A. (2016). Enneagram of personality as an
effective model in the prediction of the risk of car-
diovascular diseases: A case-controlled study. *Journal
of Cardiothoracic Medicine*, 4(3), 468–473.

Komasi, S., Zakiei, A., Ghasemi, S. R., Gilan, N. R., Veisi,
A., Bagherirad, D., & Saeidi, M. (2019). Is Ennea-

gram personality system able to predict perceived risk of heart disease and readiness to lifestyle modification? *Annals of Cardiac Anaesthesia,* 22(4), 394–399.

Lapid-Bogda, G. (2006). Developing communities of leaders through the Enneagram. *OD Practitioner,* 38(4), 57–62.

Lee, M. (2015). A study on the effects of enneagram group counseling on nursing students. *International Journal of Bioscience and Biotechnology,* 7(5), 235–246.

Maxon, B. & Daniels, D. (2008). Personality differentiation of identical twins reared together. *The Enneagram Journal,* 1(1), 65–76.

Mhunpiew, W. (2009). *Development of a career counseling center model for preparing students for the world of work using the Enneagram personality theory.* Unpublished manuscript, Chulalongkorn University, Thailand.

Mitsuda, M. & Watanabe, C. (2008). The role of the venture leader initiative in IPO accomplishment-the impact of leader characteristics on IPO performance. *Journal of Services Research,* 8(2), 141–174.

Morabito, M. (2005). *Pedagogical agents: Matching agent and learner personalities.* (Unpublished doctoral dissertation). Capella, University, Minneapolis, MN.

Nathans, H., & Van der Meer, H. (2009). The Enneagram and styles of problem solving. *The Enneagram Journal,* 2(1), 62–90.

Nayak, S. J. (2004). *Enneagram dreams: Personality styles reflected in dream content.* (Unpublished doctoral dissertation). Institute of Transpersonal Psychology, Palo Alto, CA.

Nettmann, R. W. (2013). *Moving towards, against, and away from people: The relationship between Karen Horney's interpersonal trends and the Enneagram*. (Unpublished master's thesis). University of South Africa, Pretoria.

Nettmann, R. W. & van Deventer, V. (2013). The relationship between Enneagram type and Karen Horney's interpersonal trends measured as compliance, aggression, and detachment. *The Enneagram Journal*, 6(1), 41–50.

Newgent, R. A. (2001). *An investigation of the reliability and validity of the Riso-Hudson Enneagram Type Indicator*. The University of Akron, Akron, OH.

Newgent, R., Gueulette, C., Newman, I., & Parr, P. (2000). *An investigation of the Riso-Hudson Enneagram Type Indicator constructs of personality as a unique estimate of personality when considering the Revised NEO Personality Inventory and the five-factor model of personality*. Paper presented at the joint meeting of the Association for the Advancement of Educational Research and the National Academy for Educational Research, Ponte Verda Beach, FL.

Newgent, R. A. Parr, P. E., Newman, I., & Higgins, K. K. (2004). The Riso-Hudson enneagram type indicator: Estimates of reliability and validity. *Measurement and Evaluation in Counseling and Development*, 36, 226–237.

O'Leary, P. (1994). *The Myers-Briggs and the Enneagram*. Presentation at the First International Enneagram Conference, Stanford University, Stanford, CA.

Ooten, D. & O'Hara, B. (2010). Consciousness ascending: Levels of consciousness and the Enneagram. *The Enneagram Journal*, 3(1), 33–58.

Ormond, C. H. (2007). *The effects of emotional intelligence and team effectiveness of a newly formed corporate team learning the Enneagram*. (Unpublished doctoral dissertation.) Institute of Transpersonal Psychology, Palo Alto, CA.

Palmer, H. (1988). *The enneagram: Understanding yourself and others in your life*. San Francisco: Harper & Row.

Pedersen, E. T. (2005). *The protoanalytic study of a population of opiate addicts undergoing methadone treatment: A preliminary investigation*. (Unpublished doctoral dissertation). Argosy University, San Francisco, CA.

Perry, A. K. (1996). *Leading with skill and soul: Using the enneagram and the brent personality assessment system*. (Unpublished doctoral dissertation). Seattle University, Seattle, WA.

Pop, F. C., Vaida, M. F., & Cremene, M. (2010). An alternative strategy for grouping students in eLearning using an Enneagram methodology and eye tracking. Paper presented at the 9th International Symposium on Electronics and Telecommunication.

Pratiwi, D., Santoso, G. B., & Saputri, F. H. (2017). The application of graphology and Enneagram techniques in determining personality type based on handwriting features. *Journal of Computer Science and Information*, 10(1), 11–18.

Prien, H. (1998). *The Enneagram and the actor: Using a system of personality typology in character analysis*.

(Unpublished doctoral dissertation). Southern Illinois University, Carbondale, IL.

Raitamaki, S. (2012). *How does Enneagram help in developing emotional intelligence at work?* (Unpublished doctoral dissertation). Inholland University of Applied Sciences, Amsterdam.

Randall, S. (1979). *The development of an inventory to assess enneagram personality type.* (Unpublished doctoral dissertation). California Institute of Asian Studies, San Francisco, CA.

Rasta, M., Hosseinian, S., & Algahar, G. (2012). A survey on the effectiveness of nine-type personality training (Enneagram) on the mental health (anxiety and self-esteem) of school girls. *Journal of Basic and Applied Scientific Research,* 2(11), 11845–11849.

Richmer, H. R. (2011). *An analysis of the effects of enneagram-based leader development on self-awareness: A case study at a midwest utility company.* (Unpublished doctoral dissertation). Spalding University, Louisville, KY.

Romould, E. J. (2006). *Development of an Enneagram educational programme for enhancing emotional intelligence of student-teachers.* (Unpublished doctoral dissertation). The Maharaja Sayajirao University of Baroda, Vadodara, India.

Ruffin, S. R. (2014). *An analysis of personality types as a preventative measure towards burnout among mental health practitioners.* (Unpublished doctoral dissertation). Capella University, Minneapolis, MN.

Roh, H. R., Park, K. H., Ko, H. J., Kim, D. K., Son, H. B., Shin, D. H., Lee, S. H., Jung, H. Y., & Heo, D. (2019). Understanding medical students' empathy based on enneagram personality types. *Korean Journal of Medical Education*, 31(1), 73–82.

Saeidi, M., Amiri, M. M., Ahmadi, M., & Komasi, S. (in press). The relationship between the Enneagram personality types and health responsibility in patients with substance use disorder: A brief report. *Jundishapur Journal of Health Science.*

Schneider, J. & Schaeffer, B. (1997). The Enneagram typology: A tool for understanding and counseling sex addicts. *Sexual Addiction and Compulsivity*, 4, 245–278.

Scott, S. A. (2011). *An analysis of the validity of the Enneagram.* (Unpublished doctoral dissertation). College of William and Mary, Williamsburg, VA.

Sharp, P. M. (1994). *A factor analytic study of three enneagram personality inventories and the Vocational Preference Inventory.* (Unpublished doctoral dissertation). Texas Tech University, Lubbock, TX.

Siudzinski, R. M. (1995). *Unpublished enneagram study.* (Reported in literature review of Dameyer, J. J. (2001). *Psychometric evaluation of the Riso-Hudson enneagram type indicator.* California Institute of Integral Studies, San Francisco, CA.)

Snyder, K. (1996). *Nine conflict resolution styles based on the Enneagram personality types.* (Unpublished master's thesis). California State University, Sacramento, CA.

Stevens, K. L. (2011). *Comparisons of Enneagram types and five-factor model traits of graduate psychology students*. (Unpublished doctoral dissertation). The Chicago School of Professional Psychology, Chicago, IL.

Sutcliffe, E. (2002). *The Enneagram as a model for adult Christian education*. (Unpublished master's thesis). St. Stephen's College, Calgary, Alberta.

Sutton, A. (2007). *Implicit and explicit personality in work settings: An application of Enneagram theory*. (Unpublished doctoral dissertation). University of Leeds, United Kingdom.

Sutton, A., Allinson, C., & Williams, H. (2013). Personality type and work-related outcomes: An exploratory application of the Enneagram model. *European Management Journal*, 31, 234–249.

Tastan, K. (2019). Development and validation of a personality type inventory based on Enneagram. *Konuralp Tip Dergisi*, 11(1), 112–120.

Thomas, G. (2010). Archetype and imagery in the Enneagram. *The Enneagram Journal*, 3, 59–78.

Thrasher, P. (1994). *The enneagram: Movement between types, an inventory, and a criterion measure*. (Unpublished doctoral dissertation). Loyola University, Chicago, IL.

Twomey, J. (1995). *The enneagram and Jungian archetypal images*. (Unpublished doctoral dissertation). The Chicago School of Professional Psychology, Chicago, IL.

Vaida, M. F. & Pop, P. G. (2014, May). Grouping strategy using Enneagram typologies. Paper presented at the 2014 IEEE International Conference on Automation, Quality and Testing, Robotics, (AQTR).

Wagner, J. P. (1981). *A descriptive, reliability, and validity study of the enneagram personality typology*. (Unpublished doctoral dissertation). Loyola University, Chicago, IL.

Wagner, J. P. (1994). *The Myers-Briggs and the Enneagram*. Presentation at the First International Enneagram Conference, Stanford University, Stanford, CA.

Wagner, J. P. (1999). *Wagner Enneagram personality style scales: Manual*. Los Angeles: Western Psychological Services.

Wagner, J. P. (2008). Enneagram styles and maladaptive schemas: A research inquiry. *The Enneagram Journal, 1*(1), 52–64.

Wagner, J. P. (2012). A comparison of the nine Enneagram personality styles and Theodore Millons' eight personality patterns. *The Enneagram Journal, 5*(1), 21–34.

Wagner, J. P., & Walker, R. E. (1983). Reliability and validity study of a Sufi personality typology: The enneagram. *Journal of Clinical Psychology, 39*, 712–717.

Warling, D. L. (1995). *An examination of the external validity of the Riso Hudson Enneagram type indicator (RHETI)*. (Unpublished doctoral dissertation). The University of Guelph, Guelph, ON.

Weeks, R. & Burke, D. (2009). Transforming organizations using the Enneagram: A law firm case study. *The Enneagram Journal, 2*(1), 6–23.

Whillans, P. (2009). Applying the Enneagram to the world of chronic pain. *The Enneagram Journal, 2*(1), 81–103.

Wiltse, V. R. (2000). Journeys in the night: Spiritual consciousness, personality type, and the narratives of women religious. (Unpublished doctoral dissertation). The Union Institute, Cincinnati, OH.

Woldeeyesus, B. M. (2014). *The Enneagram: Predicting consistent condom use among female sex workers.* (Unpublished doctoral dissertation). University of South Africa, Pretoria.

Wyman, P. & Magidson, J. (2008). The effect of the Enneagram on measurement of MBTI extraversion-introversion dimension. *Journal of Psychological Type,* 68, 1–8.

Yilmaz, E. D., Gencer, A. G., Aydemir, O., Yilmaz, A., Kesebir, S., Unal, O., Orek, A., & Bilici, M. (2014). Validity and reliability of the Nine Types Temperament Scale. *Education and Science,* 39(171), 115–137.

Zinkle, T. E. (1975). *A pilot study toward validation of the Sufi personality typology.* (Unpublished doctoral dissertation). United States International University, San Diego, CA.

## Related Works

*The Arica Tradition*

Ichazo, Oscar. *The Human Process for Enlightenment and Freedom.* New York: Arica Institute Press, 1976.

———. *Between Metaphysics and Protoanalysis.* New York: Arica Institute Press, 1982.

———. *Interviews with Oscar Ichazo*. New York: Arica Institute Press, 1982.

*The Gurdjieff Tradition*

Bennett, J.G. *Enneagram Studies*. York Beach, ME.: Samuel Weiser, 1983.

Blake, Anthony. *The Intelligent Enneagram*. Boston: Shambhala, 1997.

Campbell, Robert. *Fisherman's Guide*. Boston: Shambhala, 1985.

De Ropp, Robert. *The Master Game*. New York: Dell, 1974.

Ouspensky, P.D. *The Psychology of Man's Possible Evolution*. New York: Vintage, 1974.

Speeth, Kathleen. *The Gurdjieff Work*. Berkeley: And/Or Press, 1976.

Tart Charles. *Waking Up*. Boston: Shambhala, 1986.

Webb, James. *The Harmonious Circle*. New York: G.P. Putnam's Sons, 1980.

## The Diamond Approach

Almaas, A.H. *The Elixir of Enlightenment*. York Beach, ME: Samuel Weiser, 1984.

———. *Essence: the Diamond Approach to Inner Realization*. York Beach, ME: Samuel Weiser, 1986.

———. *The Void*. Berkeley: Diamond Bks, 1986.

———. *The Pearl Beyond Price*. Berkeley: Diamond Bks, 1988.

———. *The Point of Existence*. Berkeley: Diamond Bks, 1996.

————. *Facets of Unity*. Berkeley: Diamond Bks., 1998.

————. *The Inner Journey Home*. Boston: Shambala, 2004.

————. *The Unfolding Now: Realizing Your True Nature through the Practice of Presence*. Berkeley: Diamond Bks, 2008.

# About the Author

Dr. Jerome Wagner, Ph.D. is a clinical psychologist, psychotherapist, supervisor, consultant in private practice, and emeritus faculty member in the Department of Psychology and the Institute of Pastoral Studies at Loyola University, Chicago.

Among the earliest students of the Enneagram in the United States, Dr. Wagner's dissertation was one of the first written descriptions of the Enneagram and pioneered formal research studies on the Enneagram. Part of his study involved constructing an Enneagram inventory. The current version and Manual of his highly researched and statistically validated *Wagner Enneagram Personality Style Scales* (WEPPS) can be taken online at www.WEPSS.com and is available in hard copy from Western Psychological Services (www.wpspublish.com; 800-648-8857). The WEPSS is the only Enneagram inventory reviewed in Buros's Mental Measurements Yearbook (15th edition), a recognized assessment evaluator.

Dr. Wagner is the author of *Nine Lenses on the World: the Enneagram Perspective* and *The Enneagram Spectrum of Personality Styles: an Introductory Guide.* Both are available through Amazon.com.

Dr. Wagner has been researching and teaching the Enneagram since 1980 and began the Enneagram Spectrum Training and Certification Program in 1995. He has presented Enneagram workshops for business consultants and coaches, human resource directors, counselors, therapists, spiritual directors, educators, and personal growth audiences throughout the United States and in Canada, England, Spain, Finland, Australia, Hong Kong, Singapore, and South Africa.

Dr. Wagner has been an invited speaker at all of the International Enneagram Association (IEA) Conferences, was on the Board of Directors of the IEA, has been the editor of the Association's *NinePoints Bulletin*, and co-editor of *The Enneagram Journal*. He has published numerous articles in these journals as well as the *Enneagram Monthly*. For his early and continuing contributions to the Enneagram community, Jerry was honored by being named a Founder of the International Enneagram Association. He was the keynote speaker for the 2010 IEA Global Conference, the 2013 IEA China Conference, the 2017 IEA European Conference, the 2019 IEA China Conference, and the 2019 IEA South African Conference.

9 781722 505226